I0620513

# BUILD YOUR BRAND UNIVERSE

## CRAFTING A UNIQUE WORLD PEOPLE CAN'T IGNORE

## ROBYN YOUNG

THIN LEAF PRESS | LOS ANGELES

*Build Your Brand Universe: Crafting a Unique World People Can't Ignore.* Copyright © 2025 by Robyn Young. All rights reserved. No part of this publication may be reproduced, distributed, or transmitted in any form or by any means, including photocopying, recording, or other electronic or mechanical methods, without the prior written permission of the author, except in the case of brief quotations embodied in reviews and certain other non-commercial uses permitted by copyright law. The contributing authors maintain all rights to use the material inside the chapter he or she wrote for this book.

Disclaimer—The advice, guidelines, and all suggested material in this book is given in the spirit of information with no claims to any particular guaranteed outcomes. This book does not replace professional consultation. The author, publisher, editor, and organizers do not assume and hereby disclaim any liability to any party for any loss, damage, or disruption caused by anything written in this book.

Library of Congress Cataloging-in-Publication Data
Names: Young, Robyn, Author
Title: Build Your Brand Universe: Crafting a Unique World People Can't Ignore

LCCN: 2024925421
ISBN 978-1-953183-65-1 (paperback)
978-1-953183-70-5 (hardcover)
978-1-953183-64-4 (eBook)

Book Cover Design and Interior Formatting by 100Covers.
Editor: Erik Seversen, Dhanliza Cellona
Thin Leaf Press
Los Angeles

THIN
LEAF

*For Mike and Maddie.*
*Thank you for breathing life into every chapter for me.*

# Contents

.

# Introduction

Many founders and marketers mistakenly think that a brand is simply a logo, a product, or a cohesive visual design to their marketing collateral. But the reality is far more powerful.

The most successful brands don't just exist as a set of matching luggage with a consistent look and feel. They create experiences that become their own living worlds, driven by emotional connection and resonance with their audience. It's not just about having all the pieces look the same; it's about how those pieces come together.

As we've learned from Marty Neumeier, author of *The Brand Gap* among other strategy-centric books, a brand is a gut feeling or understanding about your organization, shared by you and your audience (anyone who interacts with your product or service, including customers, employees, partners, and followers).

*Put simply, a brand is how you make people feel.*

For the purposes of this book, let's make this distinction: "branding"—your logo, color palette, imagery, tone of voice, tagline, etc.—should be in service of your "brand," the space you hold in the audience's mind that separates you from competitors. While your branding helps you communicate the intended perception, it *does not* make up the heart and soul of your brand. Your brand is reflected by more than just the tangible expressions; it includes the unique language, beliefs, actions, behaviors, and experiences that make it distinct and memorable.

Brands are also no longer about dictating the perception from the top down. This shift can be uncomfortable for many because it means relinquishing some control over your brand. Your audience plays a crucial role in co-creating your brand through how they engage with, discuss, and feel about it. The goal isn't to manage every detail—it's to facilitate the brand experience alongside your audience.

So where do you start? Lead with intimacy. Become hyper-focused on who your audience is—not by measuring search queries, purchase history, or social media engagement numbers—but by truly understanding them on a deeper level. People are drawn to brands that they feel seen by. It's not about pushing messages; it's about creating a connection. Brands that show they genuinely "get" their customers are often rewarded with attention, engagement, and long-term loyalty. To do this effectively, you need to get to know them as people (not as consumers)—their quirky humor, deepest desires, most audacious dreams, or other emotional trigger points.

Your Brand Universe doesn't need to be massive to have impact. Some of the most memorable brands intentionally keep their worlds small, preserving a sense of customer intimacy and maintaining the magic that's often lost as companies pursue endless growth. By focusing on quality interactions over customer acquisition, you can foster a more meaningful connection with your audience, creating a loyalty that larger brands often find difficult to replicate.

Ideally before launching, you would gather an engaged community of potential early adopters to test drive ideas—this can be your own network of followers as the founder, tapping into an existing external network or creating one from scratch. You'll read more about this in Chapter 7: Genuine Culture. But rather than simply sitting back and waiting for the audience to tell you what the brand should be, it's imperative to also gain clarity and focus on what your own *desired perception* of the brand is. Only then can you create an authentic, sticky, and memorable Brand Universe that keeps audiences engaged and enamored with your company for years to come.

## About the Book

In this book, I will cover in detail the foundation for creating (or surfacing) a distinct brand identity, as well as how to amplify your brand through your assets, experiential touchpoints, platforms, channels, behaviors, and actions. The book includes five layers to building out a Brand Universe: Your Brand POV, Ownable Identity, Unique Experience, Narrative Amplified, and Genuine Culture. In my work as a brand strategist and creative partner to emerging startups and (largely) founder-led businesses, I have used these layers to help pull apart the facets of cohesive brand worlds in an effort to make the work of building them less overwhelming. My work comes from my experience in the trenches, helping founders to brand (or rebrand) over 70 ventures across industries, as well as years spent studying prolific brands across the globe, and countless hours digesting anything I could find on world-building in a number of verticals—including improv, fictional writing, film, gaming, and music—and how it relates to brand building.

## *Brand building is not a science. It's an art.*

This book is ***not*** meant to be a road map for your first year of business. Nor is it a formulaic system in which you can copy/paste the success of other brands onto your own. Brand building, after all, is not a science—it's an art.

*Build Your Brand Universe* is intended to be a guide you can refer back to throughout your brand building journey. Look to it to find frameworks and principles that have stood the test of time, be inspired by both iconic and emerging brands, and most importantly, to muster up the continuous passion and courage required to take action in your own brand. Because it is an ongoing pursuit. There will always be more you can do to shape the perception and experience of your brand world.

**Author's Note:** Throughout this book, I have indicated examples both of brands I've worked for and with directly, and others that I've observed and admired as a brand builder and consumer but have no direct relationship with. Some will inevitably go out of business or be canceled by the court of public opinion. The principles of the example brands I've used are not always indicative of the success of the business itself. I can't predict which brands will still be around in 5, 10, 20 years because there's more that goes into keeping a business going beyond the brand. I'm also not endorsing any bad behavior (past, present, or future) by the brands or founders I've included within.

## Why Invest in Your Brand?

Now that we have a shared understanding of what we mean by "brand," let's unpack the value of having one. Whether you are a one-person shop or an established enterprise, you presumably have customers, clients, or followers you want to develop a connection and eventually, a lasting relationship with. That relationship is built on the back of the shared perspective you have with them (i.e. your brand point-of-view). The more original and ownable this shared perspective is, the more tangible and memorable your Brand Universe will feel to all those who interact with it.

*Strong brands significantly outperform their weaker counterparts in both sales and profit margins.*

A strong brand isn't just a status symbol—it's a strategic asset that drives real financial gains. Research from Bain & Company and other sources has shown that successful brands can achieve up to 50% higher profit margins compared to weaker brands. This is largely due to the increased pricing power, customer loyalty, and the ability to attract repeat customers without significant marketing costs that established brands enjoy.

While it is possible to have a successful company built around a product, without a brand, you have a commodity. In these cases, customers will associate your company solely with your product. The challenge is that the connection is purely transactional—there's no emotional loyalty. The success of your company will be dictated by your ability to either compete on price and convenience, or remain ahead of the competition on features, enhancements, and attributes *at all times*. Once something better, cheaper, or faster comes along, your customer will be more easily swayed away by the competition.

A strong brand enhances a company's bottom line by allowing it to charge premium prices, deepen profitability per customer (rather than just borrowing market share), and increase profit margins through customer loyalty, which reduces marketing costs for customer retention. Regardless of whether or not you invest time, capital, and manpower into your brand, your business and product will develop some kind of reputation or perception over time as people become more aware of it. The question is whether you will be deliberate and intentional about shaping that perception—or not.

## Buy-in Barometer

As you build your Brand Universe, you will (in most cases) bring others along for the journey; employees, internal and external partners, ambassadors. In order for your Brand Universe to remain cohesive and continue to expand, you'll need buy-in or commitment from these collaborators as to its purpose. I've seen some of the most compelling brand strategies fail miserably because they lacked the necessary support of their people to see them through.

There are three key ingredients needed to achieve buy-in for any venture or enterprise - Clarity, Confidence, and Action. These are the internal benchmarks for successful brand building. They indicate whether or not you have what's necessary (above and beyond the logistics and deliverables) to achieve long-term results. Skip any one of these, and you're likely to experience a number of bottlenecks in establishing your brand.

- Without clarity, your team will be aimlessly firing on all cylinders. They'll have enthusiasm but not real dedication to the cause (and thus, easily swept away by shiny objects).

- Without confidence, you'll get criticism and spectatorship. Your people will understand the new direction, but they'll be waiting in the wings to see if it actually works, ready to place blame and point fingers at the slightest bump in the road.

- If you have clarity and confidence, but never take demonstrated action on your strategy—well, your brand becomes the greatest story never told, likely living in a brief somewhere, but no one on the team can tell you what the brand actually means or why it's important.

Only when you are clear and confident in your brand and take meaningful, strategic action toward it will you see the lasting results of building a Brand Universe. As you work through this book, you can sense-check yourself and your team by asking these three questions:

1. Am I/are we clear on what sets our brand (not just our product) apart from competitors?

2. How committed am I/are we to what the brand stands for? Is this what I/we care about most?

3. Am I/are we willing and able to take action on this?

# 1

# How to Build a Universe

Imagine for a moment that you could create your own reality. Like the Christopher Nolan film *Inception*, you get to be the architect, determining the unique makeup of your dream—the experience, the colors, the sounds, the people. This is not just some mythical plot for a movie. As an entrepreneur, you have the power to co-create your "world" with your customers, team members, and broader community. Most founders simply don't take full advantage of their brands in this way, missing a huge opportunity to continuously connect and engage with both new and existing customers. While already a familiar practice in the gaming industry, building a Brand Universe works well across verticals—whether you have one product or multiple, or even one entity or multiple that fit the same audience. It can be applied to both product-based or service-based businesses alike.

No doubt, as a consumer, you've experienced the lasting effects of engaging within an immersive, experiential brand world already. One of the most well-known and classic examples is Disney. The spatial planning alone within a Disney property has been studied by architects and experiential designers around the world. Each detail has been carefully coordinated to make you feel as though you are in a wonderland from the moment you step through the gates. The elaborate set designs and detailed storytelling throughout the parks reinforces the robust catalog of Disney films. Down to the use of subtle visual artifacts, like painting buildings sky blue so they blend in with the background rather than detracting from the experience within each land.

Above and beyond the visual decor and architecture, there are also social codes and behaviors that are customary only within Disney properties. When you visit any of the Disney parks, it is not uncommon to see adults in Mickey ears. This is not only acceptable but also encouraged within the proximity of Disney's Brand Universe. However, remove that person from that environment, and this behavior starts to feel strange. In fact, the further this adult is from a Disney property, the more it feels out-of-place.

World-building no longer requires you to have a physical space to accomplish this. Your Brand Universe exists in the minds of customers more than it does within the confines of four walls, a roof, and a ceiling. Your platforms can provide the "space" for your audience to interact within this world, to share common beliefs, values, interests, trends, and even goals and dreams. To find the people who think like they do. Your product can be a gift with purchase to an experience you invite them to be part of.

*Your Brand Universe exists in the hearts and minds of customers as much as it does in the platforms where they interact with it.*

We've seen examples of this, not just from brands leveraging alternative digital spaces but also from individuals, artists, and creators. Taylor Swift is one of the best examples of building a Brand Universe around music. She has her own visual and vocal language, creating a platform for her fans to engage. Not only does each album tell a story reflective of her coming of age experiences as an artist, but Taylor is also a mastermind at using Easter eggs—cryptic codes and hidden clues within her shows, lyrics, music videos, social channels, even her wardrobe at public appearances—to tease out her upcoming albums. Through her record-breaking global Eras Tour, attendees' step into a world of both intimacy and grandeur, where fans are adorned with friendship bracelets and outfits that reference their favorite Swift eras. When you enter Taylor's World, it becomes your reality. She puts her heart and soul into something that's autobiographical and launches it to an audience who feels seen by her ability to reflect their experiences within her own.

In this new landscape, the audience wants more from the brands they interact with. Customers aren't just your buyers anymore. They are collaborators, community members, co-creators building your Brand Universe alongside you. Having an engaging community is about facilitating the conversation rather than controlling it. As Jonathan Emmins points out in *Worldbuilding: The Evolution of Brand Building,* brands are no longer built in isolation by founders or marketers. Instead, world-building is a collaborative process where customers, fans, and communities shape the narrative alongside the brand. Rather than thinking in terms of campaigns and channels, brands need to think in terms of relationships and affinity. It's about creating a space where your audience feels empowered to take part in the story, transforming from consumers into co-authors of your brand world.

This means relinquishing some control. You may set the stage, but your audience will build the reality with you. The most compelling brand worlds—whether physical or digital—embrace this openness, inviting their audience to contribute and deepen their emotional connection with the brand. It's this shared authorship that makes a Brand Universe feel alive, evolving with every interaction.

## The "Game" of Worldbuilding

How does one find ownable space in which to create a compelling Brand Universe?

For roughly 20 years now, I've been a fan of improv comedy. If you follow the principles of improv, finding a distinct idea to build your brand world around is similar to finding the "game" in a scene. The goal of "game" in improv is to recognize a unique thing that comes up organically in a scene and amplify it. Rather than engineering something unique, you are *discovering* something that is unusual from the scene. It could be something your scene partner said or did, an eccentric way they moved, etc.

One example of the "game," as described to me by my Upright Citizens Brigade instructor Betsy Stover, was her observation of a local police station that looked like a medieval castle from the outside—highly unusual—and became the inspiration for a scene. For example, the people at this medieval police station wouldn't drink out of cups; they would drink out of goblets or chalices. They wouldn't eat donuts; they'd eat turkey legs. They would speak in Old English and joust and all the things you'd expect to go along with that "reality"— that becomes the premise for your scene. It supports how characters should speak, what they believe, and how they'd behave.

In brand building, we'd consider this unusual or unique thing an "insight." It could be about your audience, the industry, or the broader culture. Insights are "informed inferences," often based on observations that derive core truths about your brand. They provide fruitful territory for a bigger idea. That bigger idea should give us a sense of how we might shape your Brand Universe (just as we would shape the improv scene), identifying how things and people within that "world" would look, sound, and behave.

*Insights inform core truths about your brand identity and shape the foundation of your Brand Universe.*

I once shared this concept with a startup founder who produced homemade pasta sauce from scratch and sold it in small frozen pellets safely stored in freezer bags to keep the sauce as fresh as possible. She said to me, "My audience would never dream of eating pasta sauce from a jar. The best option would be from an antique sauce pot passed down from their Italian grandmother. The second best would be from our bags." That insight came from an interesting audience observation—identifying the distinct beliefs and actions of her core customers. She can use it to shape tangible aspects of her Brand Universe, such as packaging. Perhaps her packaging has a picture of a quintessential Italian grandmother on it. Or maybe the individual pellets come out of packages shaped like sauce pots, for example.

## Prompt: Gather Insights

1. Start with 10 interesting observations about your customers—what are their needs and/or wants? Don't be too precious about whether or not they relate specifically to your product or service just yet—you may be able to make a connection later. Focus on the emotive trigger points, positive or negative.

_____

_____

_____

_____

_____

_____

_____

_____

_____

2. What is happening in the broader world or culture that could be influencing your customers' experience as it relates to this insight? This will help you identify what the potential cause is for why your customer feels a certain way and how it relates to "what" they want or need.

_____

_____

_____

_____

_____

3. Finally, what patterns do you notice in these observations that may help you make an "informed inference" about them?

_____

_____

_____

_____

_____

## Anatomy of a Brand Identity

To create a unique Brand Universe, you need a unique brand identity. What makes a brand identity unique? Ask 10 different brand strategists and you'll likely hear 10 different answers. In this book, I will highlight eight main components that I've both used as a brand strategist and recognized in other successful brands that shape a unique and memorable brand identity.

_They are:_

❐ Human Truth

❐ Monster

- ☐ Core Belief
- ☐ Tribe Mindset
- ☐ Archetype
- ☐ Call-to-Arms
- ☐ Offer
- ☐ Vision

At the heart of your brand identity is the core belief. It sets up the point of view that provides meaning and reason for your brand, above and beyond selling products or services, acting as a gravitational pull within your Brand Universe.

### *Your brand's core belief sets up its point of view and provides the reason for why it exists (beyond selling products or services).*

Your core belief doesn't need to be a lofty social impact purpose—like world peace. It can simply be a specific and compelling motivation that you share with your audience. Think of your product or service as the anchor point of that motivation, but not the reason itself. Throughout this book, I will refer to your brand identity (or brand point-of-view) frequently, and in the next chapter, you will work through these eight components. It's imperative you don't skip this step as the strength of your Brand Universe will depend on the depth of your identity.

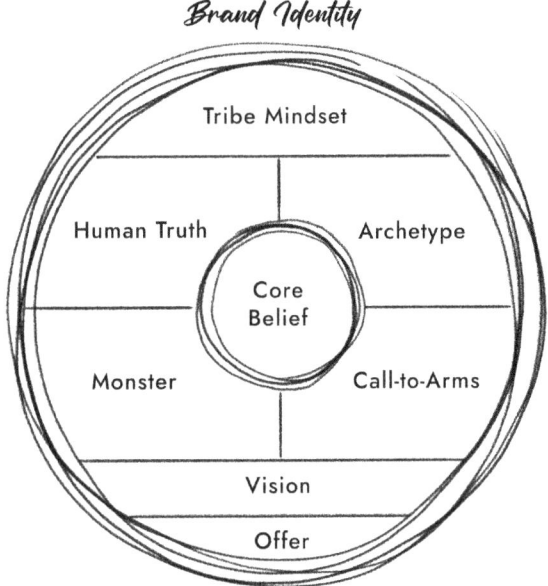

*Brand Identity*

## Amplifying a Distinct Identity

In 2003, Chip and Joanna Gaines created a unique brand identity from a simple ethos still reflected on the brand's website today: "We believe in home. But we've learned that home doesn't have to be a physical destination. [It can be] any place you feel known, loved, and always welcomed back." While the couple is widely known for renovating spaces into modern, country chic havens via the HGTV show *Fixer Upper*, the Gaines' actually started their business after borrowing $5,000 to create a single shop, Magnolia Market, the first of the Magnolia brand that would become an empire. Today, their Brand Universe occupies a number of ventures in multiple categories—a quarterly magazine, books, a home decor line, a realty firm, and a network with original programming. Effectively, fans of the brand can be reading Magnolia Journal, sipping a Magnolia coffee from a

Magnolia brand coffee mug, while sitting at a table at Magnolia Market or watching Magnolia Network from the comfort of their (likely) Magnolia-clad homes. That's brand immersion on a scale most companies can't even fathom. And it all exists under one defining identity crossing multiple categories.

Brand is often grouped under marketing because traditionally, it was seen as a function of external communications. But marketing is just one way to activate your distinct brand identity. Your identity should sit at the center of your Brand Universe, informing everything you do from the experiences you create, to the content you produce, the products and services you offer, the brands you partner with, the people you hire, the behaviors you cultivate, and everything in between.

*Your brand identity should sit at the center of your Universe, informing everything you do from marketing and communications, to experiences, content, products, and services.*

In this book, I have focused on key principles and highlighted some of the most effective tools that will help you build a distinct and memorable Brand Universe. It is by no means a comprehensive list. Nearly all of the functions of your business can be used to express and amplify your brand. Your brand identity can and should be used as both a filter and a lens for decision making across your business. The strength of your brand can be measured in the interconnectivity of your brand touchstones, and how they communicate your core belief. Don't be distracted by which "bucket" each idea fits under. The goal is a cohesive brand identity with a variety of ways to engage.

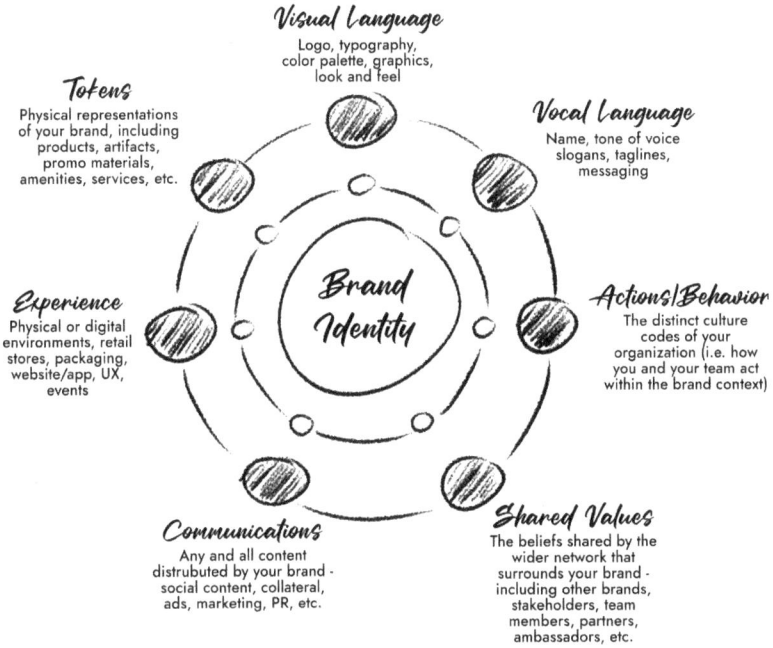

## What Makes a Great Brand Universe?

As you begin building your brand world, it's important not to get ahead of yourself and start building without understanding what the story or point of the world is. Marie Mullany, author and fantasy world builder, describes this as "world-building disease" and cautions all who are interested in crafting engaging worlds, "Only build what you need when you need it," rather than front-loading everything at once. This same principle applies to your Brand Universe. Not every brand needs a podcast, for example, nor does this format suit every brand's story. A great Brand Universe isn't created by the sheer amount of touchpoints it contains but by the richness of those touchpoints

Rather than thinking channel-first, build your Brand Universe from the inside out.

Prioritize the identity of your brand, then gradually add the platforms, media, channels, and products that will best amplify your authentic identity and provide layers for your audience to explore.

*Immersive worlds take shape over time, crafted with layers of narrative and brand personality that invite audiences to explore more deeply.*

Imagine creating touch points on a map, each with their own distinct value and opportunities for audiences to engage within your brand world. These points of interest should collectively make up a cohesive ecosystem—furthering your brand's overall ethos. (You'll learn more about this in the Think Flywheels, Not Funnels section of Chapter 5.)

The most intriguing brand worlds also have one important element in common: scaffolding. There's a certain amount of brand-regulated structure to these immersive brand environments, without feeling like a chokehold on the audience. They're not simply free-for-all places where anything goes. There are socially accepted behaviors, religious-like practices, and even rules reinforced by the brand that participants know about and *mostly* abide by. While it's important to know that people may break these rules, having them is important to create consistency with what the heart of the brand is—and why people interact with it in the first place. (You'll learn more about this in Chapter 7: Genuine Culture.)

And finally, brand worlds reflect the times and culture around them, evolving with the outside world to maintain relevance. This is why audience collaboration and input is crucial. Even in the most distinct and immersive Brand Universe, there should be a connection—direct or indirect—to the outside world. Simply disregarding the reality that your audience must live in (when they're not in your world) is the quickest way to be deemed a tone-deaf brand.

## Key Takeaways from Chapter One

1. **Find the "Game":** Identify a unique and ownable aspect of your brand or audience that can expand into a larger idea. This becomes the foundation for building your Brand Universe.

2. **Build with Intention:** Focus on defining your brand's identity first, ensuring it reflects your values and point-of-view, before selecting the channels and platforms that best amplify your message.

3. **Create a Cohesive Ecosystem:** Treat your Brand Universe as an interconnected system of distinct touch-points, each offering opportunities for your audience to engage and connect with your brand.

4. **Collaborate with Your Audience:** Invite your customers and community to co-create your Brand Universe, evolving its story and experiences through their active participation.

# 2

# Your Brand POV

When you're living and breathing the day-to-day hustle of building a company, it's easy to get lost in the details—features, ingredients, process, updates and benefits—of what you sell. You are, no doubt, intimately familiar with the ins-and-outs of your product, but your customer isn't. In fact, getting your brand noticed feels like pushing a boulder uphill. In my signature keynote entitled *The Brand Curve*, I explain this as "trying to climb the Audience Affinity Hill"—a steep climb to achieving brand awareness, creating a connection, engaging and delighting your audience, and finally reaching the Holy Grail of brand loyalty. It is not a linear path, and the climb can take years, decades even for brands to achieve (if they achieve it at all).

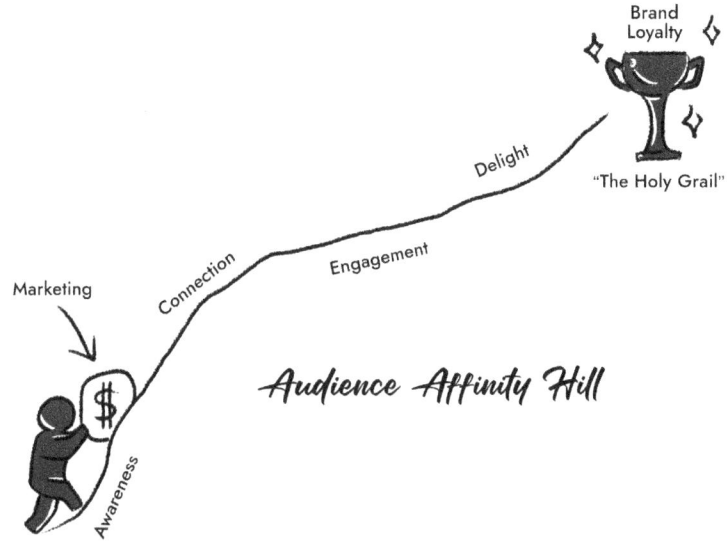

A common mistake I see companies make is leading with their product or service attributes in their marketing. They struggle to get past the awareness phase, even in cases where they have a better product. Convinced that the right funnel, or viral video, or influencer mention is their silver bullet up the hill, they inevitably get caught in the vicious cycle of spending more to make sales and following channel *tactics* rather than creating *traction* through their brands.

In a competitive market, selling on product intrinsics alone doesn't give you much leverage, especially where competitors can easily outspend the newcomers. When it comes to connecting with an ideal audience, particularly at the beginning, a bold and often polarizing brand point-of-view (POV) allows you to cut through some of the early work to get noticed.

*Your brand's point-of-view (POV) establishes the center-of-gravity of your business.*

Elevating your brand around a bigger idea or broader human desire will help you get out of the weeds of selling on your product attributes, starting from a stronger foundation that will fundamentally speak to your audience on an emotional level. Your brand's POV (i.e. your brand strategy) will establish the center-of-gravity, giving merit to why it exists (beyond selling products/services) and how it differs from the competition. It also provides the scope of your brand world, giving direction to where you should (and shouldn't) play.

In this chapter, you'll work through frameworks for identifying a brand point-of-view that sits above your products or services and any functional or emotional benefits. Identifying a compelling point-of-view gives your brand meaning (beyond the rational) and positioning power, creating space for you even in the most crowded markets.

While not every component needs to be highlighted in every campaign, piece of content, or collateral—in fact, it would be nearly impossible to do so—it's important to flesh out each of the eight components. Each component should also support the "bigger idea" for your brand POV.

As you're working through this framework, you may find that one component opens up new, fresh territory for your brand positioning that feels really different from your competitors. You may even get sidetracked with how you will execute that idea. It's okay to capture these in notes, illustrations, and thought tangents along the way –use the space in this book to jot these ideas down if it helps– but don't skip the rest of the chapter. Use each component to ensure you can support the POV. It will strengthen your confidence and clarity in your brand, and your willingness to take action in building your Brand Universe around it.

## A Human Truth

One of the best ways to build a brand that will leave a lasting impression on customers for years to come is by tapping into a "truth" or understanding about your audience. This is a prevalent framework used in both brand strategy and psychology, generally derived from an observation about your target customer, a behavior pattern that you notice in multiple customers, OR a universal truth about the human condition.

*A human truth interprets the motivation behind a consumer's needs.*

A human truth goes beyond just datasets, observations, or statements of need. It interprets *why* people behave a certain way. What is the human motivation behind those needs? You can utilize Maslow's Hierarchy of Needs here as a reference point.

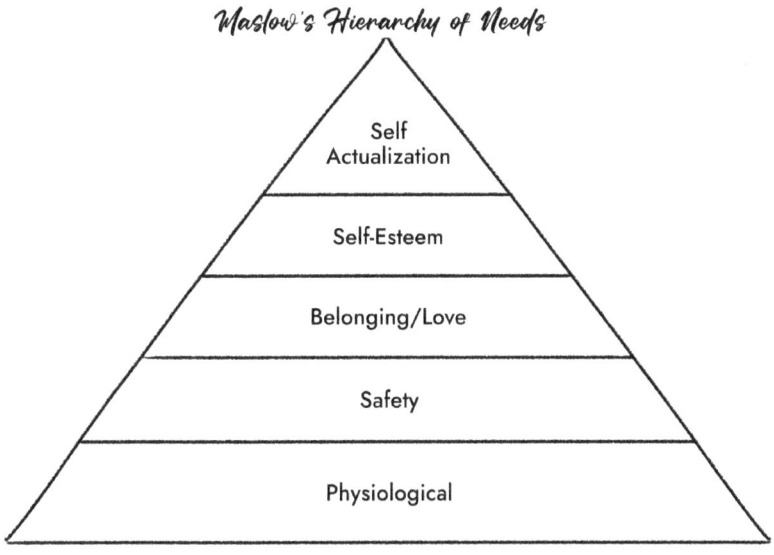

Imagine you're writing a pitch deck for your business. The human truth would be the emotive opener that gets everyone in the room nodding in agreement before you've even pitched your product. It's because humans aren't all that different. We share many of the same fears, experiences, frustrations, and desires. Sure, there's nuance around these topics, but when it comes to your brand, the best approach is to find the motivation that transcends semantics.

Airbnb is a great example of this. The brand speaks to a basic and compelling human motivation: the desire for belonging. We all have an intrinsic need to explore, connect, and feel a sense of community. The brilliance behind Airbnb's slogan "Belong Anywhere" is that it addresses the universal human desire of seeking genuine connections and experiences regardless of location. While it directly relates to travel, it resonates on a much broader level by appealing to the fundamental human desire for belonging and community.

## Prompt: Find the Human Truth

Refer to the insights you gained from the "Gather Insights" prompt of the last chapter and complete this sentence to elevate your insight into a human truth. You may need a few tries before you land on a breakthrough idea.

*People are motivated by [core human desire], which makes them long for [emotional fulfillment], leading them to want [behavior/outcome].*

Here's an example for Airbnb:

*People are motivated by the desire for belonging, and it makes them long for authentic experiences and connection, leading them to want to explore and engage with new cultures and communities.*

*Notice that there's nothing in this statement about the actual service (home rentals). This is intentional since the goal is to identify a bigger brand idea that sits above your product or service. If you're struggling to find an emotive motivation, it may be that your insights are too close to product needs. Zoom out to better understand what's driving your customer's desires.

_____

_____

_____

_____

_____

## Who (or What) Is Your Monster?

Every great story has a conflict—two forces fighting against each other: Good vs. Evil, Rich vs. Poor, Man vs. Nature, New vs. Old. It's a fundamental principle of storytelling. Think of Star Wars. Without the Dark Side, there would be no need for the Rebellion. Conflict is not only a centerpiece to every great film, TV series or novel; it is also one of the most effective ways to unlock massive competitive advantage in your brand. By embracing a monster in your story, you not only create intrigue, but it also gives your brand positioning power. When brands do this well, they create friction in their industries by drawing an invisible line in the sand and challenging both competitors and customers to pick a side.

Image: Plamdi on DeviantArt

Once you've determined what the conflict of your story is (and which side represents your brand), it helps to imagine a "villain" or group of villains on the opposing side. This could include your competitors, but it might also include brands outside of your category—anything that is a representation of who or what you are fighting against. It doesn't have to be a specific person or brand either. In many cases, a commonly held rule or behavior that you want to challenge is the monster.

## *Embracing a monster helps to assert your brand POV.*

Liquid Death, the polarizing water brand that's taken the beverage industry by storm, is a great example. The brand infamously packaged their mountain fresh water into cans that resembled energy drinks or craft beer. Because, for Liquid Death, the monster is plastic. But rather than spending marketing dollars discussing why metal is infinitely recyclable, they made their entire brand about "Death to Plastic." It's quite virtually a brand that leans into metal, from the packaging to the heavy metal music used in their videos.

In other cases, the monster is completely fabricated—a dramatized version of a single, compelling pain point felt widely by the customer base. For example, Pepper, the bra brand specifically designed for people with small busts, has taken on an enemy their core customer has been battling forever—the dreaded "cup gap." Unlike the standard bra fit complaints that many brands gloss over, Pepper has turned this unique pain point into their ultimate villain. Their battle cry "No more cup gap!" is a rallying promise that women with smaller busts never knew they needed, but now can't live without.

Occasionally, the monster can actually be the absence of something. One startup I worked with recently in the microgreens space determined that the monster in their brand was "big, drastic subtractions." A commonly held belief in the diet industry is that you need to make big subtractions from your diet to make significant progress. But this brand believed that these drastic changes led most people to give up on eating healthy. Thus, it was the "monster" in its brand story.

Thought Starter >

Who or what are you fighting in your category (or in the world at large)? Give a name to the opposing force. Who (or what) is your brand's Darth Vader, Kylo Ren, Emperor Palpatine, etc.?

Credit: rawpixel.com

## Prompt: Air Your Grievances

Here's your chance to work out all of that angsty aggression that may have encouraged you to start your business in the first place. What do you dislike about your industry? What are the "unspoken rules" in your category that you think are complete hogwash? Who is contributing to the problem (companies, people, groups, etc.)?

_____

_____

_____

_____

_____

_____

_____

_____

_____

_____

## Identifying the Monster

Understanding who or what you are fighting will help you begin to form a point-of-view for your brand, moving the focus from individual pain points to projecting a much grander narrative. Take note, there's a difference between who is a "villain" contributing to the larger enemy, versus the real "monster."

Once you've identified the monster, it becomes easier to address the conflict of your brand. This is what really gives your point-of-view longevity. Because while the villain and monster might eventually be defeated, conflicts last, and your brand is more likely to last as well if you can identify the conflict in your story.

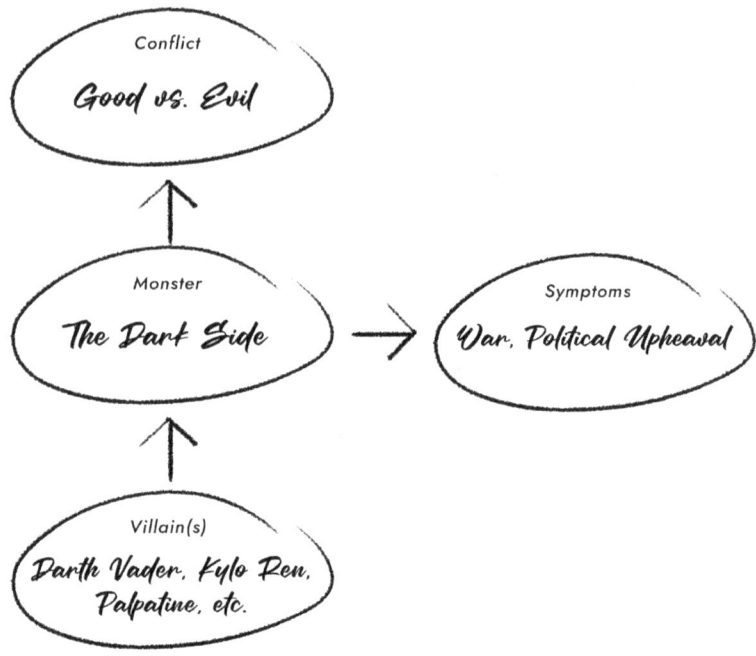

An example of an enduring "monster" can be found in the communications of digital money transfer service, Wise. While traditional banks continue to offer complex fee structures for international transfers, Wise launched a provocative campaign challenging the opaque and exorbitant fees typical in the industry. The campaign featured stark, honest messaging and real-life stories of customers frustrated by hidden fees. Prior to the campaign's official release, Wise conducted guerrilla marketing stunts, including projecting messages about transparency and fairness on prominent bank buildings. Their goal is not just to provide a cheaper way to send money internationally but also to revolutionize the financial industry by promoting transparency and honesty, taking a stand against the $200 billion in hidden fees charged by banks annually.

**Conflict:** Transparency vs. Secrecy

**Monster:** Hidden Fees

**Villain:** Traditional Banks

Similarly, on the heels of Apple's announcement of the iPhone Titanium 15, Back Market, a marketplace for refurbished devices, produced a bold parody that mimicked the tech industry's obsession with "new" and classic marketing tropes (i.e. backlit product shots and dancers choreographed with tech gadgets in hand). Prior to the spot's launch, the brand created faux ads for a more sustainable and affordable phone model and "leaked" them in high-traffic areas around Apple's headquarters. The campaign wasn't just selling refurbished tech. It was to change the way people think about tech and circularity, taking on the 50M metric tons of electronic waste produced annually.

**Conflict:** New vs. Refurbished

**Monster:** Preoccupation with the "newest gadget" in tech

**Villain:** Apple

## Prompt: Call Out the Monster

Now, it's your turn! Call out the "monster" you want to fight. Think about who is contributing to the problem (industry competitors, public figures, other groups), and find the common threat they share. Once you identify the monster, see if you can clarify your story with a single conflict. Think "this vs. that."

As you go through this exercise, you may find that you have pain points that creep back into the story again. These are almost always "symptoms" of the monster rather than the monster itself.

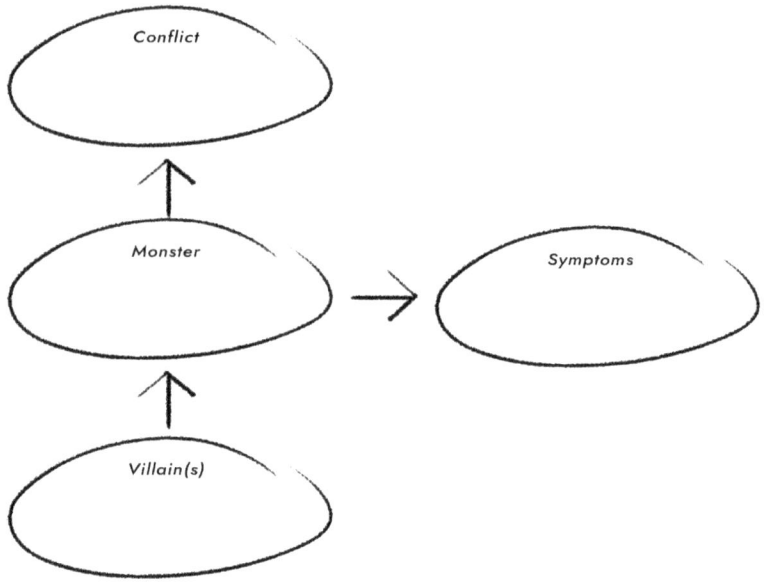

## Core Belief

In the face of our monster, what do we believe that informs everything we do?

This core belief should be more than just a generic statement; it must represent a point of view that could spark disagreement, ensuring it's not just a platitude but a genuine stance. A core belief defines your brand's ethos, guides your decisions, and sets you apart in the industry. It acts as a North Star, keeping your brand aligned with its values and resonating deeply with your target audience. When clearly articulated, a core belief can transform your brand from just another name in the market to a movement that inspires and connects with people on a profound level.

*A core belief defines your brand's ethos, guides your decisions, and sets you apart in the industry.*

This is a construct many brand strategy firms use to simplify a core belief statement:

*In a world of [describe your monster], we believe [core belief].*

Here's an example of how a brand like Vital Farms might answer that:

*In a world of <u>deceptive messaging like "cage-free" from other egg brands about how their chickens are raised</u>, Vital Farms believes in <u>honesty and transparency</u>. 'So, they keep it bullsh\*t-free.'*

That's more than a production practice; it's their core belief that informs everything they do as a brand. This commitment to straightforward, honest practices not only differentiates Vital Farms in a crowded market but also builds trust and loyalty among consumers who are tired of being misled. Their transparency about farming practices and dedication to animal welfare challenges the status quo and sets a new standard in the industry.

## Prompt: Forming a Core Belief

Return to your list of dislikes in your industry from the last section. Make a list of what the opposite characteristics would be. Find the common ground. Are there similarities to the opposite characteristics that might inform your core belief? For example, are they all related to one particular theme (trust? equality? transparency? something else?) Find any common ground that relates to your monster. Then complete this sentence with multiple answers till you find one that fits.

_____

_____

_____

_____

_____

In a world of _____ we believe _____ .

**Example:** *In a world of deceptive messaging like 'cage-free' from other egg brands about how their chickens are raised, Vital Farms believes in honesty and transparency.*

_____

_____

_____

_____

_____

## Establishing a Tribe Mindset

The standard practice of grouping customers according to their gender, location, race, or other demographic characteristics no longer fits our modern world (if I'm being honest, it has felt archaic for a while now). Customers don't always behave the way their demographic data says they "should." Consumption patterns aren't clearly defined by traditional demos like location, age, or gender. Consumers identify more as groups who share beliefs and behaviors. Those shared sense of beliefs, traditions, behaviors, and values create "tribes" that aren't specific to their gender, age, or other external factors.

This is where psychographics come into play. Unlike demographics, which categorize people based on external traits like age or income, psychographics focus on internal characteristics, such as values, interests, lifestyles, and attitudes. By understanding what drives and motivates your audience, you can create more meaningful connections with the 'tribes' that resonate with your brand.

In other words, you could have a 25-year-old male from the city and a 55-year-old female from the suburbs who are part of the same tribe because they both identify with the same beliefs. When it comes to your brand, niche audiences should then be constructed not on gender, age, income or other ancillary descriptors, but on their shared mindset. It's important to remember that a brand for everyone is a brand for no one. The aim should not be to establish the brand for everyone, everywhere who may buy the product, but instead to identify a specific shared mindset of your *ideal* target audience. Your brand should strive to be the aspirational example of that mindset as well.

### *A brand for everyone is a brand for no one.*

A great place to start when addressing who is in your camp is to first consider who is not in your camp. Who are you willing to sacrifice speaking to in order to draw in the audience that you want? For example, fast food sandwich chain Arby's seems to sacrifice potential customers who are vegetarians and vegans to attract their core audience—meat lovers. Hence, their slogan "We have the meats." The brand has gone as far as selling merch with slabs of steak imprinted upon them and cleverly turning out creative campaigns that poke fun at who they're "not for" as well. One ad, for example, simply displays the number for a 'vegetarian support hotline' with the Arby's logo. With any other brand, a set of sweats printed with carnivorous meats all over it would seem bizarre. For fans of the Arby's brand, it is just another expression of their shared love.

The Optimists campaign from the University of California, Los Angeles is another example of pulling in an audience through a mindset. The campaign has run for decades now, and it's easily one of my favorites to have personally worked on because the mindset of the audience was crystal clear. The brand managed to capture the determination, ambition, and persistence that many of their students, alumni, instructors, and employees share. Videos would show iconic figures in music, sports, science, and a number of other categories who attended, worked for, or were otherwise associated with the University—creating connection with an audience who could recognize themselves within these figures. While the demographics of their stakeholders vary immensely, the spirit of anyone who considers themselves a Bruin (the University's mascot) is what they share. It's more than just academic achievement or skill; it's an aspiration and ethos. The brand calls them "Optimists."

## Prompt: Divide the World

Part 1: One of the best ways to assert your brand point of view and attract those who share it is by drawing a line in the sand. It's almost always easiest to address who ISN'T in our tribe first. Who are we not for? What audience are we willing to sacrifice?

Part 2: As a result, who WOULD agree with our core belief, and thus is in our tribe? What is the mindset of our most ideal, die-hard advocates? Can you give them a "label" based on this shared mindset the way UCLA did with the "optimists"?

_____

_____

_____

_____

_____

## Archetype

A brand's point-of-view is not just a statement of intent—it should actively shape the actions and behaviors of the brand and how it engages its audience. When aligned with a strong archetype, the brand POV becomes a lens through which every action and interaction is filtered.

An archetype is a universal character type or personality that embodies a set of behaviors, values, and motivations. In branding, archetypes help define the "role" your brand plays in its story and how it connects emotionally with your audience. Archetypes provide a framework for shaping your brand's personality, ensuring consistency in its actions and messaging. A useful resource is Iconic Fox's list of 12 of the most common archetypes to give your brand a clear behavioral path, ensuring that its values and actions resonate deeply with your customers.

For example, a brand embodying the Explorer archetype, like Patagonia, focuses its behavior on adventure, sustainability, and freedom. Patagonia consistently acts in ways that align with its archetype by encouraging customers to explore the outdoors while taking bold stances on environmental issues.

On the other hand, the Innocent archetype, represented by brands like Dove, leads the brand to behave in ways that emphasize simplicity, purity, and honesty. Dove's campaigns often focus on themes of natural beauty, transparency, and self-care, reflecting the brand's commitment to these values.

Selecting an archetype that is vastly different from your competitors can be an easy way to signal a big difference in your brand too. For example, a small business I worked on strategy with had a 30-year history leading workshops in writing and reviewing for companies. This client wanted to stand out from their two biggest competitors who had very buttoned up, corporate brands. Our client had assumed they also needed a buttoned up brand to be taken seriously. But following their competitor's lead wasn't going to help them stand out. We determined that leaning into an Outlaw archetype was not only a more authentic representation of the witty, tongue-in-cheek energy they brought to their workshops, it was also a slam dunk to clearly separate them from their stucky corporate competitors.

## Prompt: Define Your Archetype

Discover which archetype aligns with your brand's point-of-view. Iconic Fox's list of Brand Archetypes is a great place to start (www.iconicfox.com.au/brand-archetypes). You may find that a couple of archetypes fit the direction you want to take for your brand personality. Selecting more than one archetype often allows brands to avoid clichés and stereotypes, creating greater depth and originality to the brand's personality. At the same time, too many archetypes can create confusion. To avoid diluting your brand's behavior, choose, at most, one primary and one secondary archetype. By focusing on a specific combination, your brand's behavior can remain authentic and distinctive.

_____

_____

_____

_____

_____

## Call-to-Arms (CTA)

A call-to-arms is the rallying cry that galvanizes your audience, turning passive followers into active participants in your brand's mission. This is not about crafting a catchy slogan or a memorable tagline, but about issuing a clear, compelling directive that inspires action. Think of it as your brand's ultimate call-to-action. It should be a bold statement that encapsulates your brand's core belief and resonates deeply with your audience's values and aspirations. This call-to-arms should be specific, encouraging your audience to take tangible steps in alignment with your mission.

### *A call-to-arms is the ultimate CTA for your brand.*

What action are we telling our audience to take in order to 'join us' on this mission? Try to stay away from generic statements – like 'Join the Movement'-- and aim for specificity. Be careful that your call-to-arms doesn't just reaffirm your product. "Buy More _____." is not a compelling rally cry for your audience. Here's a few examples from two very different brands:

> **TOMS - Stand for Tomorrow!** TOMS' call-to-arms focuses on social impact. By purchasing their products, customers are invited to support various global causes, from providing shoes to children in need to funding clean water initiatives.

> **Nike - Dream Bigger, Do More!** Nike goes beyond "Just Do It" with campaigns encouraging people to dream bigger and achieve more. This call-to-arms motivates their audience to push their limits and break boundaries in all aspects of life, not just in sports.

## Prompt: Lead the Charge

Imagine you are leading a protest or rally for your cause— you have no more than three to five words you can use per placard sign. What would your signs say? What are you asking your audience to DO? What would you want the crowd to be chanting at the end of this protest? Use the section below to work through your brand's call-to-arms statements that align with your POV. Ideally, they should be no more than 3-5 words per statement.

---

---

---

---

---

## Offer

One of the most common challenges founders I meet with have is communicating their offer in simple, compelling language that tells the audience what their product or service actually does. With the clarity of the rest of your brand point-of-view in place, the way in which you talk about "what" you offer should feel like the final cherry on the sundae—neatly wrapping up the story of your brand with *what* you're doing to fight the monster and back up your belief while channeling the tribe mindset and leading the charge with your call-to-arms.

### *Your offer is the punchline in your brand story.*

This is the first and only time in your brand story where your actual product or service comes into play. It's intentionally planned this way so that you no longer feel inclined to lead with product intrinsics and attributes. Your product or service is no longer the headline, but rather the punchline in your brand story.

The benefit of brevity in describing your offer cannot be overstated. I once read in Adam Grant's book *Hidden Potential* that Lin-Manuel Miranda came up with the idea for Hamilton while he was on vacation, sipping a margarita of all things. He probably wrote it out on a napkin. In fact, a number of iconic visionaries have used this very same format to communicate their ideas:

- Walt Disney sketched out his vision for Disneyland on a napkin during a family dinner.

- Herb Kelleher, co-founder of Southwest Airlines, wrote out the airline's business plan on a cocktail napkin while at a bar in San Antonio.

- George Lucas outlined his initial ideas for Star Wars on a series of napkins during a meeting with Alan Ladd Jr., the head of 20th Century Fox at the time.

The real benefit of the back-of-the-napkin is in its forced brevity. Your ability to communicate your product or service in a concise manner requires both clarity and confidence in it (read: no fluff, industry jargon, or subjective words). Entrepreneurs invest so much time into lengthy presentation decks (yep, I'm guilty of it too), but the fact of the matter is that when the offer is strong enough, it doesn't need all the pomp and pageantry.

## Prompt: Back-of-the-Napkin

While you're out to dinner or happy hour, grab a cocktail napkin and a sharpie. See if you can simplify your offer onto this 5x5 space without sacrificing appeal. If you don't have a napkin, use the square below. Ideally, you should be able to explain it within a single sentence and maybe a few key bullet points. The goal isn't to describe every facet of what you do—it's to focus on the most important pieces. Be relentless with your editing: What is absolutely essential for your audience to know to understand the value of your product or service as it relates to the rest of your brand point-of-view?

* Share your answer with me: Take a picture of your "back of the napkin" and share it on LinkedIn. Tag @robyn-young with #backofthenapkin if you want free feedback.

## Vision

What's the impression or impact you want to make with your brand? Forget about what you think is logical or practical—this is a place for BIG, audacious dreaming. In the bestselling book *Built to Last*, Jim Collins refers to this as his "BHAC framework" (Big Hairy Audacious Goal). He explains that the most successful brands set their vision on energizing challenges. Again, your ambition doesn't need to be "world peace," compelling as that may be. Choose something that is bold yet meaningful to you and your team. Here are a few examples from well-known brands:

**Google:** "To provide access to the world's information in one click"

**Tesla:** "To accelerate the world's transition to sustainable energy"

## Prompt: Brand Obituary

Imagine your brand/business has come to an end (tragically), but you have one last hurrah to pay homage to all of the work you and your team have done, the reputation you fought hard to achieve, the significant change you made to the industry (or the world at large). Write the obituary for your brand, focusing on the biggest impact that you had. This should feel audacious: think "our work isn't done until 'this' is the state of the world, our industry, our customer's lives, etc." Once you've written your brand's obituary, see if you can describe the end goal or impact into a single sentence.

_____

_____

_____

_____

_____

## Brand POV on a Page

Bring together all of your answers for each of the core components of your brand point-of-view and organize them into this one-page summary you can easily refer back to:

| | |
|---|---|
| Human Truth | |
| Monster | |
| Core Belief | |
| Tribe Mindset | |
| Archetype | |
| Call to Arms | |
| Offer | |
| Vision | |

# Key Takeaways from Chapter Two

1. **Establish Your Center-of-Gravity:** A strong brand point-of-view serves as the foundation for your business, elevating your brand beyond product attributes to reflect a bigger idea that sets you apart from competitors.

2. **Fight a Monster:** Embrace conflict to assert your POV by identifying a "monster"—a shared enemy you want to challenge—and use it to create friction, intrigue, and alignment with your audience.

3. **Draw a Line in the Sand:** Define who your brand is (and is not) for, because a brand for everyone is a brand for no one. Bold positioning clarifies your values and attracts a tribe that truly aligns with your mission.

4. **Create a Distinct Personality:** Use your POV to select an archetype that informs your brand's voice, design, behaviors, and communication styles, ensuring every interaction reinforces your unique identity.

5. **Rally Your Audience:** Develop a clear and compelling call-to-arms that inspires action and turns passive followers into active participants in your Brand Universe.

6. **Craft a Resonant Offer:** Position your product or service as the punchline to your brand story, ensuring it supports your POV and reinforces the values and mindset of your audience.

7. **Set an Audacious Vision:** Envision the lasting impact you want your brand to have, setting bold, long-term goals that inspire your team and connect deeply with your audience's aspirations.

# 3

# Ownable Identity

Too often, companies will depend on their logo as their only identifier. While logos are a trademarkable asset, relying solely on them to signal your brand to your audience is a missed opportunity for building a distinct brand world. Cover up the logo on any Hilton collateral, and it will look just like every other generic hotel brand. There's nothing ownable about their visual or vocal identity. It looks and sounds just like Marriott, Hyatt, and Sheraton. While you could argue that having a basic visual or vocal identity extends the lifeline and global use of these brands, it also requires much more effort to stand out, allowing boutique brands with recognizable character to take up space, pulling attention (and customers) away.

In this chapter, I'll unpack the most dynamic ways to energize your brand identity beyond a logo, creating a distinct and memorable set of signifiers that—when orchestrated together—will allow your audience to *sense* your brand anytime they come into contact with it. Each of these signifiers is a single tool—one is not necessarily more important than the other—yet collectively, they pack a big punch to create recognizability.

You don't need to be winning in all of these areas to be effective. The goal is to find something you can *own*, then let the rest of the elements complement it. Establish assets led by your brand POV work that will make up the foundation for your Brand Universe. Finally, socialize it with your audience, and assuming it lands, trademark it if you can.

Thought Starter >
How much are you currently depending on your logo as your only identifier?

## Brand Name

Though certainly not the only tool for building a memorable Brand Universe, naming is one of the most powerful ways to signal what audiences can expect from your brand. Entire books have been written on naming, covering everything from styles (descriptive, metaphoric, fabricated, phrase) to tactics (onomatopoeia, alliteration). Rather than delving into every technique, let's focus on a central idea: Select a name that reaches beyond your product, something that gives your brand room to grow and evolve. When creating a Brand Universe, the name should promise something beyond a single physical representation.

*A brand name can evoke a world of its own, signaling emotion, aspirations, even values.*

Take names like "Tesla," "Patagonia," or "Nike." While none of these names immediately describe a product, they offer hints of innovation, adventure, and strength, respectively. They create a foundation that goes beyond what they sell and invite customers into a larger story. Here are some essential points to consider when naming your brand:

- **Don't Tie Your Brand to a Single Product:** Your brand name doesn't necessarily need to convey what your product does. A literal name may test well with consumers who have no prior knowledge of your brand, but it may restrict your future growth if your product evolves or if you expand into new categories.

- **Evoke Emotion Over Function:** Some of the best names don't define a product attribute—they create a feeling. Names that evoke emotion or a story draw people in, acting as conversation starters. An abstract, intriguing name like Airbnb (shortened from "Air Bed & Breakfast") piques curiosity and sparks conversation, making customers lean in to learn more.

- **Balance Symbolism and Flexibility:** While names can reflect aspects of what the brand does (like "Lyft" symbolizing an easy way to get around), they should also give enough space for audiences to interpret and form their own connections. A name that's suggestive rather than prescriptive leaves room for deeper brand storytelling and a unique culture to evolve over time.

- **Positioning Your Brand as a Destination:** Some names convey a sense of place or feeling that lets people "step into" the brand. For instance, Patagonia evokes rugged terrain and exploration. This positioning gives the brand room to grow into different product categories while always staying true to its adventurous spirit.

Thought Starter >
What are the top 3 characteristics you want to convey in your brand name? List other names, people, places, or phrases associated with these qualities that resonate with your core audience.

## Product Name

Founders often miss the mark with extending the brand personality to their product names. Even in cases where the brand name has depth and story, they'll assign generic, descriptive names to their products and services. A thoughtful approach to product naming extends your Brand Universe even further. Product names should reinforce the overall brand message and, ideally, carry some of the same emotional resonance as the brand itself. Here are some examples of brands creating evocative product names that align with their brand worlds:

- **Satisfy,** a French running brand, uses poetic and atmospheric names like GhostFleece, CloudMerino, and CoffeeThermal for its high-performance apparel. Each product name not only describes the product's attributes but also evokes a feeling or state of being, inviting runners into a brand world that's rooted in mood and experience.

- **Drybar** brings its playful brand personality into its product names. Items like Three Day Bender, The

Double Shot Oval Blow Dryer, and Hot Toddy Heat Protectant are memorable, fun, and convey specific benefits without feeling clinical. Each name is an opportunity to add character and build on the brand's identity.

## Prompt: Name the Baby

Imagine your brand is the parent and your products/services are the babies—part of the family unit that is your business. You would never give your baby a generic name like "Third Child," even if that is technically what they are. You'd choose a name with meaning, perhaps inspired by what personality you can imagine they'd have in the future. Just like naming a child, you want your product names to have personality and meaning (beyond the obvious) to form their own identities. How might you rename any generic product/service to give it character that connects with your brand POV?

_____

_____

_____

_____

_____

## Visual Language

Every founder is acutely aware they need a logo for their brand. But many fail to go beyond a logo when establishing their branding. Your brand's visual identity extends beyond your logo-mark to include a number of treatments, colors, images, icons, or animations that—when orchestrated together—make up a detectable visual language.

## *Your brand's visual identity extends far beyond your logo.*

When these elements are distinct and consistent, they create familiarity without needing to depend on a logo. When working with clients on visual language at my company Young & Co., we often design the logo last—defining colors, typefaces, and design treatments first to ensure that the entire visual system communicates the brand's essence and creates a robust, memorable presence—not just the logo.

Consider Apple's minimalist design language, which emphasizes clean lines, neutral color schemes, and ample white space across all touchpoints, from its product designs to its retail stores. This understated yet sophisticated style reinforces Apple's brand positioning of innovation and elegance. For eyewear brand Warby Parker, a warm color palette and playful illustrations establish a recognizable brand feel. When orchestrated together, these elements create an identity that customers can spot instantly, whether online or in-store.

Occasionally, products themselves can carry enough recognition that they become part of a brand's visual identity. In the case of LEGO, the primary colors and iconic shapes of the toy manufacturer's classic rectangular building bricks are globally recognized. You do not need to see the brand's insignia in order to immediately recognize their IP, even when it's out in the wild. It takes years, decades even, to reach this level of discernibility.

However, new brands can channel this strategy by ensuring that there is more to their visual identities than a logomark and maintaining a reasonable amount of consistency as they continue to introduce new products and build out their brand worlds.

Image: LEGO bridge in Wuppertal, Germany - Copyright Morty on Wikimedia

## Mood

One of the best ways to begin translating your brand point-of-view into a visual, experiential language is through moodboarding. This is a branding technique that uses collaging to communicate potential "directions" or moods for your brand. Start with imagining the vibe you're trying to evoke with your brand. Is it whimsical and dreamy? Edgy and provocative? Modern and funky? The essence of your brand should reflect the archetype, personality and point-of-view as it sets the tone for how your audience will interact with your Universe.

## Prompt: Create your moodboard.

1. Start by mining keywords from your brand strategy—particularly any that relate to a feeling, your brand POV, or words associated with your brand's archetype. Select two to three that will become the essence of your brand.

2. Use the photo sharing app Pinterest to start a secret board and name it your brand's name.

3. Begin collecting images that "feel" like your brand. This can be anything that reminds you of the brand you want to build—photos, graphics, textures, color swatches, etc. I recommend using magazines, print materials, collateral from other brands (outside of your industry) that you admire, and found imagery rather than just sourcing from Pinterest (which can often lead you down the path of same-sameness).

4. If you're drawing a blank, try to imagine your brand appealing to the five senses: what it would look like, smell like, sound like, etc. You can also imagine attaching it to a physical object (challenge yourself to pick something other than your product). Here's some examples to get you started:

   If your brand were a shoe, what would it be?
   If your brand were a song, what would it be?
   If your brand were a cocktail/drink, what would it be?
   If your brand were a place, where would it be?
   If your brand had a smell, what would it be?

_____

_____

_____

_____

_____

## Iconography

Dating back centuries when hieroglyphics were used by Ancient Egyptians to identify their possessions, to the Medieval era when elaborate coats of arms were drawn to distinguish between the statuses of different nobilities, we have made use of iconography that signifies an identity. When it comes to creating icons for your Brand Universe, aim for originality in your industry by contextualizing your difference with a specific aesthetic. Think about how companies like Google use colorful, distinctive icons for all of their apps not just within their platforms but across customer experiences, creating a unified and recognizable brand no matter where you interact with them.

*Icons are more than just illustrations; they are part of the fiber of your brand world.*

Another example of classic iconography in the Nintendo Universe is the renowned video game Super Mario Brothers. Within the Mushroom Kingdom, the icons are as recognizable as the game itself, from Super Mushrooms to coins, Koopa Shells, Fire Flowers, and whatever that box with the question marks is. Visit the Super Nintendo World at Universal Studios in Hollywood and you will experience how the brand's expansive set of icons have become legendary in their own right, recognizable to even non-gamers as part of the Super Mario Universe. These are more than just illustrations; they are part of the fiber of your brand world.

Image: Super Mario Bros. Icons at Super Nintendo Land, Universal Studios

## Color

Tiffany's... Glossier... Duolingo... Barbie. These are all brands that have so religiously honed in on their hues, that they effectively "own" the colors that are associated with them. Once the brand becomes a household name, the color takes on a life of its own. Ask any marketer what "Tiffany Blue" is and they can pick the swatch out of a lineup. Glossier made Millenial pink what it is today with the brand's use of the tone across packaging, social media content, and overall experience. Duolingo's bright shade of green is as recognizable as its beloved owl character. And the Barbie movie sent shock waves of bubblegum pink on every social platform for months before and after the premiere. These brands are so closely related to their signature colors to the point that you don't even need to see the colors, and yet your brain will be able to recall them to memory. To change even the tones of these brands is to strip away part of their identity.

*Color imprints memory, anchoring your brand in the minds of audiences and creating a visual signature that's hard to forget.*

This owned-color strategy works best when it is a single, specific, deliberate tone that extends beyond the obvious logo color palettes, it's the dominant (and dare I say overwhelming) color across a brand's ecosystem—Instagram grid, packaging, office space, mascots, etc. That said, you can also choose a well-orchestrated palette of colors to create your brand identity if you are not aiming to "own" a single hue.

Thought Starter >
Colors are often associated with emotions—in fact there is an entire psychology around the use of certain colors to evoke a feeling. Revisit your brand POV answers to see if you can identify one emotion you aim to evoke with your brand. Is there a color commonly associated with that emotion that you can own in your space?

## Typography

Every typeface has its own voice. The selection and pairing of typefaces (or fonts) can create a dynamic overall impression across your brand communications. Many brands will purchase fonts to avoid using typefaces that are more widely used, and the extra savvy brands will work with a font designer to create a completely original typeface. If you're at the beginning of your business, investing in an original typeface may not be the best use of your funds; however, you should be mindful that the free/cheap fonts used represent your brand appropriately.

### *Fonts change the context in which we receive messages.*

Think of the last time you visited a fine dining restaurant or a luxury hotel. The fonts used everywhere from the menus to the signage to the keycards evoked a quality that aligned with the vibe of that establishment. The same is true for your Brand Universe. Fonts change the context in which we receive messages. As comedian Don McMillan points out for us in his stand-up bit "Font Choice Matters," the Declaration of Independence would not have been taken seriously if it were written in Comic Sans.

*You'll always be mine*

**YOU'LL ALWAYS BE MINE**

## Fonts matter.

If you're working with a designer, they can select typefaces or fonts that pair well with your logo and brand archetype, but it can be helpful to know if there are certain styles that you gravitate toward.

Thought Starter >
Determine two to three brands that feel like they have the same (or similar) energy to yours. Add examples of these fonts to your mood board. You can also use resources like Fonts in Use (www.fontsinuse.com) or Font Pair (www.fontpair.co) to learn which fonts pair best with each other.

## Brand Photography

Before audiences read your website, social post, email, or any other collateral piece, they will see it. In that split moment, they often decide whether to go any further based on the imagery alone. Photography plays a crucial role in building a distinct and memorable brand identity. It tells a visual story and gives the audience snapshots into the brand world you're inviting them to explore. Depending on what you are selling, your brand may need a mix of product and lifestyle photography. Both types should work in harmony to tell a unified story and evoke a consistent feeling across all touchpoints. It's also important to consider where the images will appear—from social media to e-commerce and ad campaigns—and tailor them to fit each platform without sacrificing cohesion.

While stock websites have become popular for brands needing quick, inexpensive visuals, they have also contributed to the homogenization across industries. That's because companies often gravitate toward the same photos, and while your viewers may not specifically recognize the images as stock, they sense the lack of originality. Stock imagery does little to set your brand apart from competitors. The more unique your images are, the more customers will recognize your brand and associate certain values or emotions with it.

### *Consistency in visual style, tone, and subjects creates familiarity.*

The key characteristic of your imagery is that it authentically represents the distinct point of view of your brand. Consistency in visual style, tone, and subjects helps create familiarity without the need for logos or text. We've all seen what happens when brands conform to category trends: a "sea of sameness" emerges where individuality used to live. Think of watch brands, where polished shots of stainless steel against muted backdrops are repeated endlessly, or water brands, each capturing similar outdoor scenes with pristine lakes or mountaintops. By avoiding generic compositions and instead focusing on original perspectives, brands can set themselves apart.

One brand that does this exceptionally well is the London-based cycling brand Rapha. Rather than focusing on flawless product displays, Rapha captures the spirit of cycling through authentic, on-location photography. They meticulously work with cyclists of all levels to showcase the world through their eyes, often photographing subjects during long-distance rides that capture the raw, unpolished moments. This approach brings out the essence of the sport, allowing audiences to feel the grit, determination, and beauty of cycling that Rapha champions. It's this commitment to authenticity that shines through, making Rapha's imagery both memorable and emotionally resonant.

## Prompt: Plan Your Photo Story

Before shopping around for photographers to work with, you'll want to get clear on your brand identity concept—how will imagery further support your brand expression? What are the unique stories you want to tell with your brand world? Your brand identity concept will also help determine the photography style, subject matter, mood, and treatment for your imagery.

_____

_____

_____

_____

_____

_____

_____

_____

_____

_____

## Verbal Language

One of the most engaging yet grossly underutilized characteristics a brand can have is its voice. You can have the best product on the market, but if your brand sounds like a robot reading a grocery list, you're going to have a tough time connecting with your audience. How your brand's emails sound, the voiceover track on your videos, the 404 error page on your website, these are all examples of and opportunities for brand voice, establishing personality and style of communication. The best brands use their voice to inject personality, create connections, and stand out from the competition.

Take acne prevention brand Starface, for example. The brand's copy reads more like a DM from a TikTok creator than a traditional skincare brand. Starface's entire brand voice is built around their quirky mascot, Big Yellow, a charming yellow cube with a face who narrates all of the brand's social content in the first person. Big Yellow's voice is as informal as it gets, peppered with memes, abbreviations, and pop culture references that make the brand's content as relatable as it is entertaining. Even their CTAs reflect this playful tone, with phrases like "Blast Off" instead of the standard "Subscribe Now." By making acne treatment feel less clinical, Starface is reorienting how skincare brands can (and perhaps should) communicate, and resonating with their young audience.

*Using brand voice is an effective way to gain early traction for your brand.*

Sorry Nonna, the pasta sauce newcomer that's giving traditional Italian sauce the middle finger, launched with a bold, irreverent tone, claiming to love their Nonna (Italian for grandma) but declaring that her recipes had become boring. So what did they do? They "stole" her recipe and spiced it up. Sorry Nonna's brand voice is punchy, playful, and not afraid to ruffle a few feathers. Their Instagram, featuring a granny flipping the bird, perfectly sets the tone. It's a refreshing take in a category that often feels stuck in the past. By injecting humor and attitude into their messaging, Sorry Nonna is already standing out in a sea of traditional brands within the space.

## Prompt: Brand Personified

To determine your brand's tone of voice, revisit your brand archetype from the first chapter. Imagine your brand as a character from a book, a movie, a play, or a celebrity. Give them a name, a gender, an occupation, a clothing style. Describe how your brand persona would talk. What kinds of words would they use? What might their inflection (pitch, pace, volume) sound like? Write out a few key phrases your company uses, then rewrite them in your persona's voice.

_____

_____

_____

_____

_____

# Key Takeaways from Chapter Three

1. **Create a Signature Style:** Develop a cohesive and recognizable brand identity that extends beyond the logo, incorporating distinctive typography, colors, imagery, and a consistent voice to make your brand universe instantly recognizable across all touchpoints.

2. **Amplify Through Storytelling:** Use elements of your identity—names, icons, and visuals—to amplify your brand POV and emotionally connect with your audience. Think beyond products to evoke values, aspirations, and experiences.

3. **Design an Ecosystem of Signifiers:** Build a cohesive system of identifiers that work together to reinforce your brand's identity and create a self-sustaining brand universe.

4. **Name with Purpose:** Choose brand and product names that evoke emotions, tell stories, and signal your broader brand POV. Avoid tying names too closely to specific products, ensuring room for growth within your brand universe.

5. **Prioritize Authenticity Over Trends:** Avoid blending into the "sea of sameness" by breaking industry conventions, and selecting design elements that authentically represent your brand's distinct personality.

# 4

# *Unique Experience*

Worlds are created in a variety of media and art forms: books, videos, digital real estate, retail environments, events, games, even performance art. There's no shortage of platforms that can be used to wield your imagination into an immersive experience. Which channels or media types you should use will be led by the products or services you're selling and the vision you have for how audiences will interact with your world. What is important is how that immersive experience will be unique to your brand, and engage your audience with multiple access points. As you're co-creating your brand with your customers, think beyond the products themselves as the only (or the ultimate) touchpoint but rather the *icing on the cake* to a greater experience.

In this chapter, we'll focus on the main touchpoints that make up your customer's journey once they're within your Brand Universe, where the intent is engagement along with surprise and delight. Chapter 6 Narrative Amplified will focus on organic content, campaigns, activations, and other marketing platforms meant to amplify your message and drive awareness, attention, and yes, traffic to your Brand Universe. While many would correctly argue that these are also part of establishing your customer journey (and thus your overall brand experience), we've separated them to differentiate between the purposes of each—Unique Experience = engagement, surprise and delight. Narrative Amplified = awareness, attention, recognition.

## Think Flywheels, Not Funnels

One of the most profound and exciting changes about modern consumer behavior is the shift away from a linear funnel model—with one entry point and one intended destination—toward a flywheel model. The flywheel concept, first coined by Jim Collins in *Good to Great*, replaces the traditional sales funnel by focusing on creating momentum through a cohesive brand engine. In the funnel model, companies emphasize customer acquisition, filling the top of the funnel with sales and marketing efforts and narrowing toward the bottom to drive conversion, then rinsing and repeating. This linear approach overlooks today's more complex purchasing dynamics. Nowadays, customers take their time to make decisions, often following brands on social media, doing their research, reading reviews, and engaging online long before making a purchase.

*A flywheel creates more momentum and engagement than a funnel.*

The flywheel model, by contrast, revolves around a synergetic ecosystem that fosters ongoing engagement and growth by prioritizing customer delight, satisfaction, and retention. By focusing on a continuous cycle of positive customer experiences, brands encourage loyalty and word-of-mouth promotion, effectively turning satisfied customers into brand advocates. In this model, your customers become part of your sales force, helping to drive the company's growth organically.

A powerful example of this approach in action is Disney's Synergy Map, a carefully orchestrated system that centers on storytelling across all its touchpoints, creating a self-sustaining, interconnected Brand Universe. Each of Disney's touchpoints— from TV shows, films, and merchandise to theme parks, music, and publishing—works in harmony with the others, each fueling interest in Disney's stories. For instance, a Disney film release not only attracts ticket sales but also drives demand for merchandise, soundtracks, and Disneyland attractions based on that film. This symbiotic relationship ensures that no matter where audiences engage with Disney, they are pulled further into the Brand Universe, reinforcing their connection to Disney's storytelling across multiple platforms.

When building a holistic brand ecosystem, you can't always predict when or where audiences will enter your Universe. Thus, your flywheel should have multiple points of contact that collectively create a synergetic experience, enhancing each stage of the customer journey. These points of contact shouldn't simply be replicas of one another. Instead, they should be consistent with the brand yet distinct in how they add value to the overall experience.

## Prompt: Sketch Out Your Flywheel

Create a list of any existing channels, high-value evergreen content, correlative products, programming that amplifies your competitive edge, and experiences that have **already** shown significant traction with customers. It could be a branded newsletter, event series, an online community, a podcast, a YouTube series, a book, or an official program. If you're just starting out, brainstorm potential touchpoints that complement your main product or service and drive attention to your brand POV. Aim to refine and focus your attention on which platforms are most *essential* to attract, engage, and delight your customers. Two to six components on the flywheel is a great starting point. Anything more than that and you're probably overcomplicating it. *If you don't yet have a full flywheel, that's perfect. Use the upcoming chapters to gain inspiration for how you can expand (or refine) your brand's touchpoints.

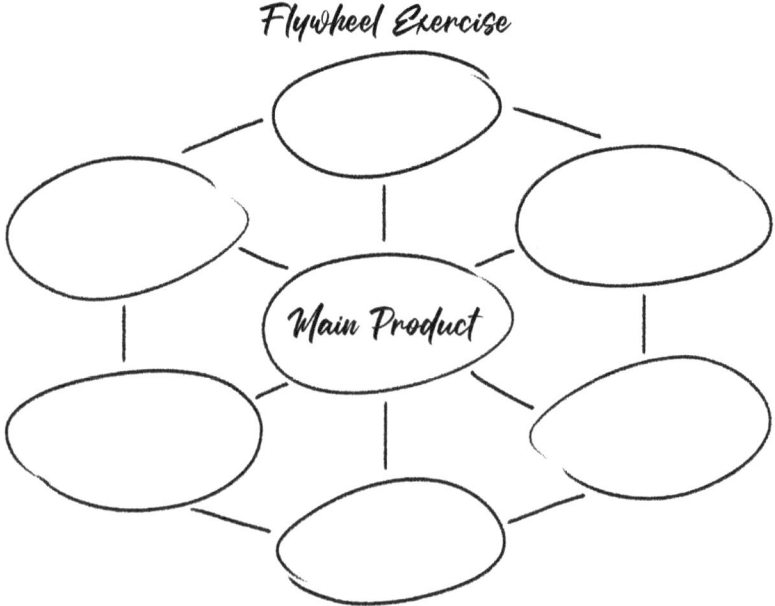

Flywheel Exercise

Main Product

## Sensory Touchpoints

Humans are sensorial creatures, storing memories based on our five senses: sight, sound, smell, touch, and taste. When designing the experiential touchpoints in your Brand Universe, consider how you can appeal to multiple senses for your audience, not only to create a more robust immersive experience but also to ingrain that impression in their memory. The more senses you engage, the more vivid and lasting the experience becomes, building stronger emotional connections between your brand and its audience.

To activate brand loyalty, sensory experiences must resonate with your brand's vibe. Smell, for instance, can be a powerful tool for brands looking to create memorable in-store experiences. Anthropologie achieves this through its signature Volcano scent, filling each of its retail spaces with a recognizable fragrance. The scent has become so popular that customers associate it directly with the brand and can purchase it to bring the Anthropologie experience home, reinforcing the brand connection in every-day life.

Sound is another impactful sense that can enhance brand identity. Mastercard spent two years creating a sonic logo, a short melody that encapsulates its brand identity and plays globally in its campaigns and retail spaces. The signature melody is engineered to adapt to various cultural settings, creating a familiar auditory presence for Mastercard customers worldwide. By engaging auditory memory, Mastercard extends its brand identity beyond the visual, making it accessible even in sound-focused environments like podcast ads.

*Engage the senses to deepen memory and connection: The more senses you involve in your brand experience, the more vividly it lives on in your audience's mind.*

Visual elements remain fundamental in establishing brand identity, but immersive, tactile experiences can amplify this. Sneaker brand Presentedby takes an inventive approach to sight and touch at its Riyadh store in Saudi Arabia. Customers walk through a flowing artificial waterfall and experience a unique mineral compound coating the sneakers, giving the impression of water cascading over the products. Presentedby's stores in London and the Middle East embody this theme, celebrating the intersection of sneaker culture, art, and design. This tactile engagement turns sneaker shopping into a multisensory experience, immersing customers in the artistry and craft associated with the brand.

Brands can also use taste in unexpected ways to enhance the brand experience. Popular card game Cards Against Humanity recently launched clam-flavored mayonnaise on Target.com. Inside each jar were 30 exclusive new cards and quirky prizes—all clam-themed—ranging from pearls to "Clam-o-merch" and even a Toyota "Clam-ry." While clam-flavored mayo might seem like an odd choice, it's a fitting, on-brand extension of Cards Against Humanity's playful, wacky world, offering customers an interactive experience that brings their humorously offbeat brand to life.

Incorporating sensory elements into your experiential touchpoints helps create a holistic Brand Universe where every interaction, whether visual, auditory, olfactory, or tactile, reinforces the brand's identity. When each touchpoint is thoughtfully designed to appeal to multiple senses, the experience becomes an unforgettable journey that resonates long after the moment has passed.

Thought Starter >
Which of the five senses (sight, sound, smell, touch, taste) could create an opportunity for your brand experience that you're not currently leveraging?

## Packaging

Imagine it is a friend's birthday, and you have worked diligently for months, or years perhaps, to find the perfect gift for them. Something you want them to know you've put considerable thought and time into. Would you then go wrap that gift in bubble wrap, encased in a plain brown box with cheap foam peanut shells and no card?

Unless your brand is ironically bucking the basics of brand building—which in itself is a branding choice—packaging is one of the most essential ways to build customer experience. Make no mistake, the customer's perception of what is in the box will be impacted by the packaging, shipping box, inserts, and inner packaging it comes in. It helps to think of it as wrapping a gift for your customer—a token of appreciation for buying a ticket to your Brand Universe—rather than a means to an end.

*Packaging is more than just a vessel; it's an invitation into your Brand Universe, reinforcing the story and experience you want to share with your customers.*

Consider BarkBox, a subscription service delivering monthly boxes of dog toys and treats. Each box is meticulously themed, with packaging that tells a story and creates an immersive experience for both dogs and their owners. For example, their "Muttcracker" box featured designs inspired by the classic ballet, complete with toy characters and treats that align with the theme, transforming the unboxing into a shared adventure. Similarly, German apparel brand StayCold draws customers into its intricate world of avant-garde tattoo streetwear by using tattoo artists to design not only their clothing but their packaging design as well with patterns and illustrations that mimic the brand's vibe.

Product packaging can also be a strategic way to stand out from competitors. Beyond design elements like color, fonts and graphic treatments, consider how you can rethink the entire shape, form, and materials. Newcomers like NuStrips are disrupting their industries, not just with new products but also with unique packaging concepts. NuStrips' fast acting paper-thin strips—which carry two to three times the nutrients of pills or gummies—aren't stored in the plastic bottles consumers are accustomed to, but in individual packets in a colorfully designed box that fits easily into your medicine cabinet.

For both product packaging and the shipping experience, the magic is in the details. From the hierarchy of the text, to the form and shape itself, brands have been made (and killed) by the seemingly ancillary choices on their packaging. Particularly for new CPG brands that must compete on shelves for attention, customers will make split-minute decisions and inferences about your product by the way the packaging makes them *feel*.

Packaging should reflect the values of your brand in form, shape, function, and materials. If your brand is committed to sustainability, every component of your packaging should be eco-friendly—or better yet, regenerative. Take Sway, a Bay Area-based company that designs innovative, compostable packaging from seaweed. Their seaweed-based materials don't just reduce plastic waste; they replenish the planet by leveraging the regenerative power of seaweed, a renewable resource that sequesters carbon, promotes ocean health, and can be harvested sustainably without depleting ecosystems. Sway's seaweed packaging is designed to biodegrade in as little as four to six weeks, making it a far more planet-friendly alternative to traditional plastics that can take centuries to decompose. By embracing regenerative design, Sway is pushing beyond sustainability to create packaging solutions that actively restore the environment, providing a clear example of how packaging can align with and even amplify a brand's values.

> Thought Starter >
> If you could choose only one impression or emotion you want to leave your customers with via your packaging, what would it be?

## Physical Spaces

Like many young adults in the early 2000s, I worked in retail. My experience included everything, from market research (interviewing customers about their in-store experience), to customer sales and merchandising (actively participating in building the brand experience). I worked with and for a number of iconic retailers—Nike, Target, Nordstrom. But perhaps the biggest impression came from my time spent at Abercrombie & Fitch.

Already a die-hard fan of the brand, I was smitten when I got the call that I was hired to work for the retailer at my local mall. Day after day, dressed head-to-toe in Abercrombie, I would walk through the double doors, past huge black and white posters of models rowing or playing football, the whiff of A&F perfume filling the air, and carefully curated pop-music playlists blaring through the speakers. Many retailers at that time focused on function in their planning of store environments, concerned with simply showcasing merchandise. A&F focused on immersing shoppers into the brand's lifestyle. I didn't know it at the time, but I was getting a crash course in retail world-building.

Though Abercrombie & Fitch has since rebranded—finding new life after a period of toxic behavior from leadership was exposed to the public—the brand pioneered a new generation of multi-sensory retail environments. They created an experience for shoppers that amplified the A&F lifestyle through visuals (sight), music (sound), aroma (smell), and textures (touch). Like most great brands, it divided audiences. Some detested A&F's stores, but many more loved it and bought their merchandise religiously.

*Brands are using their physical spaces to highlight their brand difference, elevate customer experience, and immerse visitors into their unique worlds.*

Today, brands from Dyson to Netflix are creating fully immersive environments that invite customers into their worlds.

Reinventing the way cleaning devices were displayed in department stores, stacked high with no information on how to use the machines, Dyson models its demo stores like sculpture galleries with clean aesthetics and Dyson tech displayed as art pieces, while customers try out all of the brand's latest gadgets. Other retailers like Lush use the design of their spaces to make a point about their brand difference. Lush offers handmade bath bombs and body care with food-grade ingredients like fruit, avocado, and seaweed. In designing their spaces, the cosmetics brand drew inspiration from bakeries where customers were accustomed to freshly made products, putting merch in bins with chalkboard retail signs displaying the scents.

Beyond creating immersive environments, Mox Boarding House elevates the experience by combining retail with social interaction and entertainment, crafting spaces that feel like vibrant communities in their own right. As part of the Card Kingdom brand, Mox Boarding House caters to tabletop gaming enthusiasts by offering not only a wide selection of board games like *Magic: The Gathering* and other gaming supplies but also operating as a game library and restaurant. With locations in Oregon, Arizona, and Washington, Mox creates a social hub with daily events where players can meet new people by joining in games such as *Dungeons & Dragons or Warhammer 40k* while enjoying themed cocktails and seasonal dishes. The blend of retail and gameplay creates an environment that encourages community engagement, expanding the gaming community and offering an experience beyond what online shopping could ever provide.

Image: Mox Boarding House: Portland Location - Photographer: Gummi Ibsen

## Prompt: Steal with Pride

Can your brand borrow practices from outside of your industry to create a new kind of experience for your customers that's wildly different from your competitors? Think of Dyson treating its products like an art gallery would, Lush pulling inspiration from bakeries rather than conforming to typical beauty retail standards, or Mox combining retail with a social hub for gamers. Be intentional about the decisions, they shouldn't be different just for different's sake, but should fit with your distinct brand POV in a way that serves your customers.

_____

_____

_____

_____

_____

## Workspace

Post-pandemic, the world is adjusting to a new reality of increasing popularity in (and demand for) remote or hybrid work circumstances. This creates tremendous opportunity for emerging companies to reimagine what a workspace means for them. Brands like MUD/WTR have experimented with combined retail and work environments—the alt coffee supplier's Santa Monica location calls itself "MUD/WTR: gather" and describes the space as "a cafe without the coffee, a mindfulness studio without the noise, and an open work space" all in one. The location functions as a retail space where customers can explore and purchase MUD/WTR products, but it's also designed to be an open, communal space where both MUD/WTR team members and the public can gather.

In cases where a physical workspace is required (or desired), the most beloved brands pay attention to designing workspaces that reflect their unique POV and inspire their team members. These are not just places to transact with cubicles and fluorescent lighting anymore; they are representations of the brand and reflections of the team culture. Workspaces should provide a balance of function and form, displaying the personality of the brand, with intricate details that surprise and delight visitors.

*Workspaces are not just places to transact; they are representations of the brand culture.*

For the ride-hailing company Lyft, the design of the San Francisco headquarters reflects the brand's vibrant and whimsical attitude. Features include a secret door behind a painting of Gene Wilder as Willy Wonka (one of the founder's favorite movies of all time), leading to a speakeasy-style study room, miniature parklets including live herbs and plants on each floor, and a decked-out history room where visitors can see pictures and hear stories of the early days of Lyft.

These work environments also provide opportunities for visitors to interact with your brand's IP. For LEGO's campus in Billund, Denmark, visitors are treated to the iconic bricks as well as LEGO characters throughout the sprawling 54,000 square meter space, providing a playful and collaborative environment that inspires team members to develop high-quality play experiences.

Image: MUD/WTR: gather location in Santa Monica, CA

While Lyft and LEGO's budgets may look dramatically different from yours, the principles remain the same whether you have a 54,000 square meter campus or a small office in a coworking space:

1. **Create a space that tells a story** - whether that's showcasing the history from the start of your brand, or referencing fictional characters (or iconic figures) that embody your brand.

2. **Use personal touches to add soul to the space** - the most prolific spaces have brand-personality-driven elements that often come from the founders, like the Willy Wonka references in Lyft's headquarters.

3. **Incorporate design decisions that deliver on your brand values** - whether it's open collaborative spaces or unique elements that inspire creativity, your workspace should embody the principles you stand for as a brand.

Thought Starter >

Which of the three principles for creating an engaging workspace will you implement for your space? Any ideas for how you can make the idea unique to your brand?

## Digital Spaces

In today's landscape, where an individual can gain widespread recognition from a single TikTok and multi-million dollar businesses are created off of the success of YouTube content, it has never been simpler to launch a brand without a physical location. (Note though, "simple" does not make it easy.) From interactive websites and engaging social platforms available to all on the internet, to virtual worlds available to only VR headset owners, brands are building immersive experiences for their audiences without some of the limitations of brick-and-mortars. Chief among them are the constraints that come with the laws of physics. In the digital and virtual worlds, armed with skilled designers, you are often limited only by your imagination.

## Websites

While many brands are bi-passing websites altogether these days, favoring TikTok shops and other social selling apps that allow users to buy directly from social profiles, websites still offer tremendous opportunity to do more than just inform customers and sell products. Your brand's small corner of the web builds trust and legitimacy for your company. A recent Blue Corona study found that 48% of people stated that a website's design is the primary factor in determining a business's credibility. It's an evergreen space for your customers to engage with your brand— wherever they might be in the world. It also has the potential to stoke the rumor mill and get people talking about your brand from the get-go.

Creativity goes a long way when designing a digital playground for your customers. At the same time, that creativity should serve a purpose - creating a specific impression that you want viewers to walk away with. Let's say your product is a mattress, and you want to make a point about your brand's commitment to sleep. Rather than just showing photos of the product and discussing the materials and features, could you take a page from web design agency Isadora and design a website that viewers need to "wake up"? Isadora's purely interactive landing page offers a simple game of trying to wake up the website. Tickle it, poke it, play it music, that site will not wake up, until finally, a popup screen delivers the punchline. It gets the brand point across in a playful and interesting way, drawing attention and engagement from viewers. Sure, the audience may need to be led towards another page where they can get more information and actually shop your product, but it creates a lasting impression for your brand.

*By balancing creativity and functionality, you can turn your corner of the internet into a digital playground that sparks curiosity and leaves a lasting impression.*

Storytelling is another often overlooked component to building a compelling digital space that draws your audience in. Newcomer tequila brand Casa Malka launched its site as a single-scrolling landing page with a rotating image of their beautiful glass bottle and a poetic monologue that immediately put their audience into the story with, "You wake from a dream, and you listen." Followed by a tantalizing tale that takes place in the dessert with hummingbirds and a goddess-like figure carrying you to a marble palace, the brand cleverly crafted their site as an invitation to an imaginary world it calls "the Queendom" through a well-written soliloquy and a single call to action "Join the Waitlist." Using bold typography and simple yet effective interactions, this single-scroll web page paints a captivating picture, delighting potential customers before the product is even open to the public. That, my friends, is effective brand building in digital form.

Your site doesn't need all of the bells and whistles, or to utilize the most cutting-edge web technology to delight your customers. Some of the best websites I've seen have minimal interfaces and use simple interactions to engage viewers. Balancing creativity and function is key as performance (speed, usability, load times) can suffer greatly if your site isn't carefully optimized for dynamic web content. Not to mention the number of times your website will likely need to be updated over time. Unless you are selling website design as a service, your customers will appreciate a site they can navigate through with ease while they interact with your brand.

Thought Starter >
Think on what the point of your site is in the larger context of your brand world. What role should it play? Is it the main destination for customers, or a stopping off point? What's the impression you want to leave viewers with when they visit your site?

## Social Media

While your website or e-comm shop provides an evergreen touchpoint into your Brand Universe, your social media channels are dynamic portals into your world, functioning as both a place to stumble upon your brand and to regularly interact with it. Websites are mostly static communication tools, but social media profiles are dynamic. You can learn a lot about brands in the comment sections of posts these days. How your brand responds to comments on your own posts, as well as other posts, is just as much a part of your brand as the content you put out. While many brands will jump on social media trends, topics, sounds, and cultural moments to gain attention, the best brands use their channels to amplify their unique personalities and only incorporate trends when they naturally align with that personality.

> *Social media is a stage to amplify your brand's personality and build audience connection, not just to sell your products.*

One brand that has done a particularly remarkable job with building a Brand Universe on social media is Duolingo. Millions of people are tuning in to watch the brand's beloved owl character Duo and his latest shenanigans—an impressive feat for an educational app. It's because the brand's social media platforms focus mainly on entertainment and engagement rather than selling. What's worked well for Duolingo are the ongoing gags, like Duo's hilarious crush on pop singer Dua Lipa or the character's rivalry with Google Translate. It's not just about jumping on trending sounds or TikToks for the brand, although there's plenty of that as well. Duolingo has storylines and content series that keep their community engaged and continually coming back for more.

Startups today are using social media to invite audiences into their brand world and build community before there's even anything to sell. Good Girls Snacks, the funny and irreverent Gen Z-centric brand that's making pickles look sexy, began posting to Instagram, engaging with their audience, even selling merch like their "Hot Girls Eat Pickles" hats months before launching. The brand built resonance early on by leveraging trends like "hot girl summer" and "girl dinner" that fit well with both their product and their personality. It wasn't forcing the trends to fit the brand; it was recognizing what already aligned with their audience and using it to shape their vibe.

*A word of caution: This can be a useful way to connect early on with potential customers, but trends are short-lived. Make sure that your brand isn't hanging its entire identity on a fleeting social media moment.

You needn't worry about having a presence on every social media platform at the beginning. Doing so often means you are spreading yourself and your resources too thin, sacrificing the time and work required to truly engage with your audience. Remember, build what you need when you need it. It is far better to go all-in on one channel where you can have the greatest impact with your brand. Whether it's selecting a platform where your audience is, and perhaps your competitors aren't doing a great job of engaging them. Or determining the best vehicle for the type of content that serves your brand identity. We'll cover content in more detail in the next chapter: Narrative Amplified.

## Tokens (Amenities and Gifts)

When I began working for General Assembly – a disruptor in tech education that teaches students career-building skills in new-age topics—I was immediately impressed by how thoughtfully the brand handled swag for both students and employees. Within two years, I had accumulated a collection of branded items, from a fleece jacket and GA backpack to a coveted Everlane overnight bag. But what stood out most was how these items weren't just about branding. They felt like tangible pieces of the GA culture, thoughtfully designed and given at key moments, allowing people to take a part of the brand with them, like souvenirs from a memorable trip. It wasn't the sheer amount of swag that mattered; it was the way it was integrated into the experience, turning these tokens into something more meaningful.

This kind of thoughtful gifting can be seen in a number of beloved brands as well. Away, for example, does more than just sell high-quality luggage. In fact, when the company launched its preorder during the 2015 holiday season, production was delayed. But rather than simply notifying their first customers that the product would not arrive in time for Christmas, the brand created a one-of-a-kind travel-themed coffee table book to ship to customers who had purchased luggage, creating excitement around the brand and something for purchasers to wrap up as gifts in time for the holidays.

### *Thoughtfully designed tokens turn everyday items into meaningful extensions of your brand experience.*

Another great example is Ollie, the fresh dog food delivery service that transforms what could be a simple pet necessity into an experience that delights both dogs and their owners. In the early days of the brand, Ollie included items like a branded dog bowl, serving spoon, and a custom placemat with your dog's name on it. This level of personalization deepens the connection between the brand and its customers, while also weaving Ollie into the daily rituals of their lives in a tangible, memorable way.

Similarly, Haus, the direct-to-consumer aperitif brand, elevates its customer experience by offering branded glassware and stylish cocktail recipe cards with each purchase. These gifts feel intentional and considered, turning a simple transaction into something more; they're designed to enhance how customers enjoy the product and ensure that Haus becomes an integral part of their social gatherings. It's not just about selling a bottle but about providing the tools that make the entire drinking experience feel curated and meaningful.

In these cases, the branded tokens don't just reinforce the company's identity—they extend it—making the brand feel more present in the customer's everyday life in ways that are useful and memorable. What makes tokens feel special is their inherent value within the environment they're given. Whether that value is in the status, its exclusivity, or just an extension of the brand experience, your audience should be able to recognize these gifts and amenities as something special—a kind of currency in your brand world.

## Prompt: What's Your Brand Currency?

Imagine you could create tokens in your brand world that may not hold much monetary value on the outside, but would have your audience clamoring for access. What would they be genuinely thrilled to receive? It can be extensions of your products (like in Ollie's personalized dog mats or Away's coffee table book) but shouldn't be the products themselves. Think beyond the generic brand stickers and T-shirts with your logo on them.

_____

_____

_____

_____

_____

_____

_____

_____

_____

## Products and Services

The products and services your brand offers are extensions of the overall brand experience. When done right, they don't just exist as standalone items to be purchased; they become part of the story, further immersing your customers into your Brand Universe. In his book *The Experience Economy*, Joseph Pine argues that products and services are no longer enough on their own—customers today seek memorable, meaningful experiences. In this context, your product or service should be seen as the "gift with purchase" to the experience you create around it.

For example, Peloton's exercise bike isn't just a piece of workout equipment; it's a gateway to a fully immersive fitness ecosystem with a personal, engaging, and social experience. The bike connects users to live instructors, on-demand classes, and a vibrant community of riders. Peloton uses the bike to invite customers into a larger journey, reinforcing the idea that their product is the entry point to a much bigger world.

*Your product or service is the "gift with purchase" to a bigger experience you create in your brand world.*

The design and functionality of your products should also reflect the core values of the brand. Sustainable shoe and apparel brand Allbirds exemplifies this by ensuring that every aspect of their product—down to the materials and minimalist design—aligns with their sustainability mission. The shoes, crafted from natural materials like merino wool and eucalyptus, are a direct expression of the brand's values. When customers purchase and wear Allbirds, they are participating in the brand's commitment to environmental responsibility, making the shoes more than just footwear—they become a symbol of a broader movement.

Personalization within your product deepens the connection between the brand and your customers. Prose Hair Care offers a fully customizable experience, inviting customers to co-create their own formulas based on their unique hair type, lifestyle, and even environmental factors. This level of personalization turns the product into a bespoke experience, making customers feel that the brand understands and serves their individual needs. By giving customers ownership over their product, Prose fosters a deeper emotional connection, transforming the product into something more than just a generic solution.

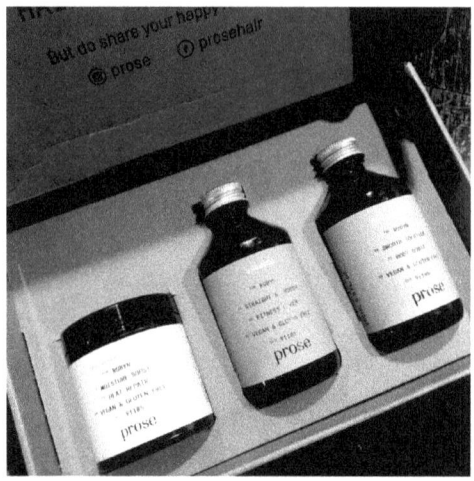

Image: My Prose personalized haircare system

In each of these cases, the product or service goes beyond its functional role. It becomes part of a larger experience, allowing customers to feel more connected to the brand. Products and services, when thoughtfully crafted, become portals into your Brand Universe, giving audiences an experience they want to return to again and again.

## Key Takeaways from Chapter Four

1. **Think Flywheels, Not Funnels:** Move beyond the traditional linear funnel to a flywheel model, focusing on ongoing engagement and delight that transforms customers into advocates who fuel your Brand Universe.

2. **Leverage Multi-sensory Touchpoints:** Engage your audience's senses—sight, sound, touch, smell, and taste—to create immersive experiences that resonate deeply and leave lasting impressions.

3. **Blend Digital and Physical Realms:** Use your brand's online and offline spaces to immerse your audience in a cohesive experience. Digital platforms offer boundless opportunities for creativity, while physical spaces create tangible connections through multi-sensory environments.

4. **Packaging as an Invitation:** Treat packaging as an extension of your Brand Universe, creating an immersive narrative that extends the brand's personality into the unboxing experience. Every detail, from materials to inserts, is an opportunity to reinforce your brand's values.

5. **Tokens with Intrinsic Value:** Create branded tokens, gifts, or amenities that feel like natural extensions of your Brand Universe. These items should carry inherent value—whether through status, exclusivity, or personalization—allowing your audience to take a piece of your brand world with them.

6. **Products as Gateways:** View your product or service as the "gift with purchase"—an entry point to the larger, immersive experience of your Brand Universe. Use it as a means to captivate your audience and invite them deeper into the unique world your brand creates.

# 5

# Narrative Amplified

As you build your cohesive Brand Universe, how do you drive awareness and attention to it? The traditional way of reaching audiences is through advertising. However, with the acceleration of ad avoidance—especially among younger generations—relying on ads may not be the most efficient (or effective) way to attract your people anymore. A study by Nielsen found that 64% of consumers are intentionally skipping ads, opting for ad-free environments as often as possible. While I'm not writing off advertising altogether– there's plenty of research to support the success of social media ads and direct response is still an effective tool for driving trial in most cases. But for the purposes of this chapter, I'll focus on the complement to paid media: earned and owned media.

There's no shortage of channels and platforms through which to amplify your brand story—social media, email, press, events, and beyond—effectively inviting your audience to experience your brand world. The real challenge lies not in using every available channel but in selecting which platforms best serve your particular audience, while staying true to what defines you as a brand.

In this chapter, we'll explore both traditional platforms used in new ways, as well as modern platforms, with inspiration from brands who have leveraged content, partnerships, user-generated contributions, and other various media and channels in distinctive ways. Whether it's through social profiles that take on a life of their own, activations that stop people in their tracks, or campaigns that spark a movement, this chapter will help you consider how to amplify your brand's voice in a way that resonates.

## Original Content

Creating content today is not like it was 10 years ago (or even 5 years ago). While AI has made content easier to produce, it has also saturated the internet and social platforms with an excess of short-form and long-form videos, blog posts, podcast episodes, and more. Most content goes unseen, which can make new brands reluctant to spend much time producing it. Yet content creation remains one of the best ways to amplify and test your brand while gaining early traction. In this crowded environment, the focus shouldn't be on creating content just for the sake of posting *something*. It should be honing content that reflects your brand's distinct personality and determining the formats that get the best engagement.

*The best content doesn't just inform—it captivates, entertains, and amplifies your brand POV.*

Every piece of content—whether it's a social media post, newsletter, article, or video—should ideally reinforce your brand's point of view. At the very least, it should reflect the unique personality of your Brand Universe so that audiences know what to expect from you. Early on, as you're still shaping your brand identity, it may take time to find your voice—this will also require a fair amount of testing. A solid copywriter/designer duo can help shape that voice, especially for startups that lack internal creative resources.

How do you determine the best content for your brand? A classic pottery class experiment offers a useful lesson. Half the class was told to create as many bowls as possible, while the other half focused on creating just one perfect bowl. Surprisingly, the group that made the most bowls also produced the highest-quality pieces. Why? Because quantity leads to quality—consistency in experimentation leads to refinement. Brands that aren't afraid to create, fail, and iterate often end up making the most authentic content. The key is iteration—learning what works and leaning into it rather than pumping out content in a vacuum.

Take the Savannah Bananas, for example. This baseball team gained national attention not just for its on-field antics but also for reinventing the game itself with Banana Ball, a new version of baseball with unique rules—like counting fan-caught foul balls as outs. The Bananas became a TikTok sensation by showcasing clips from their wildly entertaining games—from choreographed dance routines between innings to players pitching on stilts. These moments turned their exhibition games into sold-out events across the country. Founder Jesse Cole said, "We are obsessed with experimentation and trying new things every night. While most of these ideas fail, we often find gold in just a couple...and that's all we need." By embracing the mindset that quantity leads to quality, the Bananas have created a distinct brand personality that thrives on creativity, entertainment, and connecting with their audience.

Liquid Death, on the other hand, has built an expansive brand world by embracing edgy, counterculture video content. The water brand launched with a low-budget video—before their now-iconic cans had even been produced—using dark irreverent humor to challenge the traditional wellness and hydration messaging of the water category. With the tagline "Murder Your Thirst," Liquid Death's first viral video became the blueprint for their entire content strategy. The company doesn't need to jump on the bandwagon of trends to gain traction because their brand personality is already audacious. They are not afraid to create unapologetically polarizing content that repels some audiences because the brand accepts that, by doing so, they're furthering a distinct identity that their target audience already loves. By combining humor and horror film aesthetics, Liquid Death has disrupted traditional beverage marketing, amplifying their brand narrative far beyond their product.

Chubbies, the men's shorts brand, also exemplifies how low-fidelity content can help build early traction. Founded by four Stanford grads, Chubbies set out to make "thigh liberation" part of the modern man's wardrobe. But what truly set them apart was how they engaged their audience. After selling out their initial vintage-style shorts at a beach party in Lake Tahoe over Fourth of July weekend, the brand tapped into their early success by producing humorous, grassroots content that captured their carefree "weekend-warrior" vibe. Stunts like real-life Mario Kart races helped Chubbies build a community by producing lo-fi, funny content that championed relaxation and enjoyment. This content made Chubbies' brand identity more than just a product offering—it became a lifestyle.

Crafting original content isn't about production quality, but about consistency, experimentation, and staying true to your brand's personality. By iterating, testing, and refining, you'll be able to create content that resonates with your audience, amplifies your brand's point of view, and draws people deeper into your Brand Universe. Whether it's capturing entertaining pieces of your brand world, tapping into your customer's dark sense of humor, or showcasing carefree antics, the key is authenticity and a willingness to keep creating until you find your gold.

## Prompt: Plan Your Brand Content

Here's a short framework for brainstorming content ideas that deliver on your unique brand point-of-view and personality. This simple planning tool allows you to sense-check existing platforms and channels you are using (as well as new ideas you have) to determine when, where, and how your brand should show up so that you don't fall into the trap of producing trendy content that has nothing to do with your brand. Be intentional about why the channel you've selected is the best platform for amplifying your brand POV, what formats and creative execution you will use, and who will be the subject of the content (will the founder or team members narrate? Will you partner with influencers? Lean into user-generated content?). And finally, why is it relevant to people (what insight or cultural relevance does it have—pull this from your work in the chapter on Your Brand POV). Once you've identified a few concepts, create a number of different iterations that you can test (remember quantity creates quality). Finally, after posting all content, see which formats and concepts performed best with your target audience and iterate on these ideas.

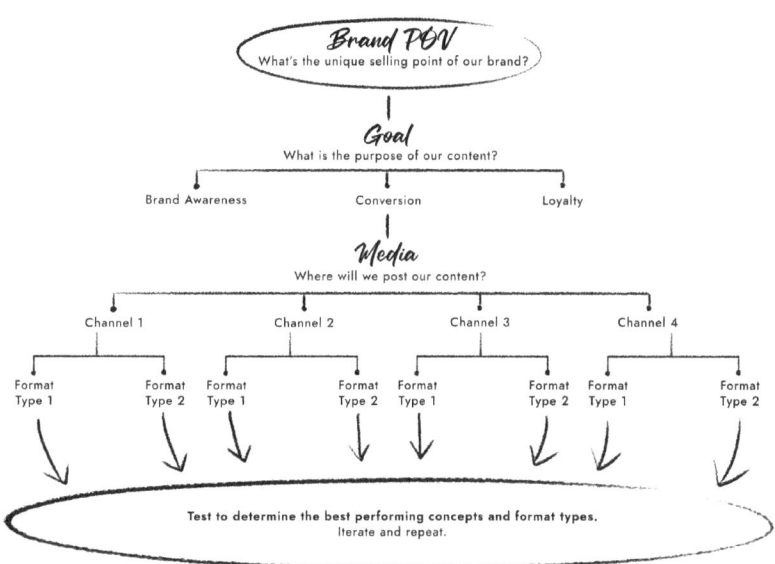

## Events and Activations

One afternoon, I was on a spontaneous day trip to Long Beach when my husband and I stumbled across a spectacle unlike any other I'd seen. From afar, we saw groups of people launching eccentric, homemade, human-powered flying contraptions off a platform into the water. The event, which drew hundreds of thousands of spectators, was Red Bull's Flugtag, a kind of air show where teams build flying machines out of found materials and attempt to take flight for mere moments before plunging into the water. Hosted in cities all over the world since 1992, Flugtag is more than just an entertaining competition—it's an event that showcases the spirit of Red Bull's brand: adventurous, creative, and high-energy risk-taking. Even as unplanned spectators without any context, we were captivated by what we were experiencing, which built recognition between us and the brand. Red Bull's Flugtag highlights how brands can turn an event into a massive, memorable experience that invites people to engage within their brand world, even in cases where they've never interacted with it before.

While Flugtag is a high-ticket example, the true magic of the event lies in its originality, creativity, and ability to leave audiences with a lasting impression of the Red Bull brand. Many startup brands assume that experiential marketing is reserved for large, established companies with extensive resources to execute elaborate ideas. But the beauty of events is their flexibility—they can be tailored to smaller budgets while still delivering powerful experiences. Whether it's a low-budget pop-up shop, a quirky competition, or a co-branded activation, experiential events give new brands the chance to make a bold, impactful statement, amplifying their uniqueness and creating a meaningful connection with initial audiences.

*Events and activations transform your brand into an experience that audiences can see, feel, and remember.*

A great alternative to planning a full-scale event is to create brand activations, which offer more focused, interactive experiences that can still have a significant impact. One brand that successfully used activations to engage audiences early on is Glossier. Originally an online-only skincare brand, Glossier embraced experiential marketing IRL through branded pop-up shops. These smaller activations created immersive environments where customers could physically engage with the brand. Their Summer Fridays Showroom in New York featured a multi-sensory experience called the Escape Room, where visitors were greeted with soft lighting, soothing sounds, and clean, fragrant scents that reflected Glossier's fresh, minimalist aesthetic. Products were thoughtfully displayed to encourage playful exploration, while Instagram-worthy backdrops provided visitors with an opportunity to capture their own moments of beauty. Every detail—from the custom playlists to the calming aroma—was carefully curated to immerse attendees in Glossier's Universe. More than just promoting simplicity and beauty as self-care, the space created something for their audience to aspire to: the Glossier girl—fresh-faced, confident, and effortlessly chic.

Events and activations can also be highly effective at driving local business on a budget. I once worked with a family-owned auto repair shop—an industry not typically known for building emotional connections with customers—to develop on-brand event ideas that would engage the local community. One successful event the business produced was a Trunk or Treat around Halloween, where attendees enjoyed a festive, community-driven experience that made customers feel like part of the family. I also worked with the team to brainstorm concepts like a classic car show paired with an animal rescue event, where attendees could bid on driving a classic car if they agreed to adopt the dog it was paired with. While these ideas centered on community events, they also served as activations that reflected the brand's unique view of caring for your car like you would a pet—emphasizing its longevity and importance to the owner.

Regardless of the scale, producing brand events and activations should not be seen as mere marketing tactics. When done well, they're immersive, bite-sized versions of your Brand Universe, forging emotional bonds and lasting impressions with your audience. Whether it's a quirky competition, a pop-up shop activation, a classic car show, or a co-branded experience, events and activations allow your brand to stand out in the digital age. The goal of any brand-hosted experience should be to provide a place where attendees can experience your brand personality firsthand and connect with people who share your distinct point of view.

Red Bull Flugtag Stockholm Sweden July 2010 © Bengt Nyman

## PR Stunts

Another effective way to generate buzz around your brand is through well-executed PR stunts. These attention-grabbing moments not only create earned media—rather than purchasing it—they also leave a lasting impression on audiences by reflecting the unique and memorable world your brand inhabits. A well-crafted PR stunt should create tension, teasing out your point-of-view to draw people further into your brand world. Done right, stunts can turn a momentary event into a lasting sensation, reinforcing your brand's identity and making a statement that resonates far beyond traditional marketing.

A famous example of this is Banksy's self-shredding artwork. Ever the anonymous prankster, during a Sotheby's auction in 2018, moments after one of Banksy's pieces sold for over $1 million, the artwork began to shred itself in front of a stunned audience. The stunt wasn't just shocking—it was perfectly aligned with Banksy's rebellious, anti-establishment persona. It amplified his distinct message, generating global headlines and leaving a lasting impression that continues to shape his brand identity as an artist.

*A bold PR stunt can turn a fleeting moment into an unforgettable statement about your brand.*

Another striking example was the World of Warcraft stunt from 2014, where a giant ax appeared to have smashed through a New York City taxi in the middle of Times Square. This creative spectacle blended World of Warcraft's iconic fantasy world with reality using a recognizable brand asset to create friction. By bringing the game's world into the real world, the stunt grabbed attention and drew people deeper into the brand's universe— showing the effectiveness of leveraging distinct storytelling and memorable brand elements to create impact.

While these examples worked well for brands that already had some recognition, PR stunts can also help boost unknown brands. For Who Gives A Crap, the eco-friendly toilet paper company, a bold and unconventional PR stunt allowed the brand to gain massive traction and initial funding before anyone had heard of them. Founder Simon Griffiths live-streamed himself sitting on a toilet in an empty warehouse, pledging not to get up until the company had raised $50,000 via crowdfunding. It took 50 hours, but the stunt was a success, meeting its fundraising goal and earning the brand significant media coverage on a nominal budget.

## Prompt: Stir the Pot

Whether through humor, surprise, or disruption, PR stunts are about breaking expectations and giving your audience something they can't ignore. To use this strategy, think of ways to create friction that aim for fame. Start by asking: How can you build agitation or curiosity through your brand point-of-view? Is it through an element of surprise (Banksy example)? Could you personify and dramatize the monster in your point of view (World of Warcraft example)? Or perform an audacious act using elements that connect to your brand identity (Who Gives a Crap)? Make a list of all of the possible ways you can stir the pot for your audience by turning the volume—and the drama—way up.

_____

_____

_____

_____

_____

## Partnerships and Collaborations

Who you choose to collaborate with says a lot about your brand. Whether through sponsorships, creator partnerships, or brand collaborations, these alliances can help shape your brand identity and expand your audience. Some partnerships are so aligned with a brand's ethos that they become a natural extension of its world, while others rely on creativity and surprise to create traction. Either way, partnerships and brand collaborations are a powerful way to build credibility, reach new audiences, and generate interest in your brand world.

Take Tracksmith, the cult-favorite running brand that proudly celebrates the amateur athlete. Tracksmith's partnerships are a reflection of this belief—they've intentionally decided not to sponsor professional athletes, instead funding aspirational amateurs. This bold move reinforces their commitment to the everyday runner and sets them apart from other sportswear brands. By staying true to their brand point-of-view, Tracksmith deepens their connection with a dedicated community of runners who value grit and personal achievement over accolades.

Meanwhile, Liquid Death, known for their irreverent branding and viral videos, has also mastered the art of unexpected collaborations. In one standout partnership, they teamed up with Martha Stewart to create a hilarious campaign promoting candle sets shaped like dismembered body parts. The humor of pairing the OG home decor expert with the edgy, anti-establishment vibe of Liquid Death made the collaboration memorable. Equally successful was their limited edition Liquid Death x e.l.f. Cosmetics kits, featuring cleverly branded products like "Thirst Quencher" face mist and "Deathly Glow" highlighter, bundled in coffin-shaped packaging. The collection sold out almost instantly, proving that when it comes to collaborations, creativity (and a bit of shock factor) goes a long way.

### The right partnerships spark curiosity, captivate new audiences, and extend your brand world.

On the flip side, brand collaborations at a product level can also be a strategic way to reach new audiences, boost recognition, or even create viral buzz. For example, Erewhon, the upscale health food store beloved by celebrities, CMOs, and wellness influencers, teamed up with Vacation Sunscreen, a brand known for its nostalgic 80s beach vibes, to create the Erewhon Vacation Sunscreen Smoothie. This unexpected blend of skincare and food tapped into the wellness lifestyle, offering customers a smoothie packed with skin-boosting ingredients like collagen and coconut water, all wrapped in Vacation's playful retro aesthetic. The collaboration was quirky, fresh, and honored both brands' distinct personalities, drawing in curious health nuts and beach lovers alike.

Then there's the delightfully bizarre brand partnerships that toe the line between collaboration and stunts. For instance, the partnership between Velveeta and Nail Inc., where the two brands entered the beauty world with cheese-scented nail polish. The limited-edition Pinkies Out nail polish encouraged Velveeta consumers to "live rich" and embrace a decadent lifestyle. Though the scent of cheese might not be to everyone's taste—the playful collaboration certainly made headlines and reinforced Velveeta's cheeky, indulgent brand identity.

These examples show how partnerships and collaborations can extend a brand's reach and provide a fresh way to engage with both loyal and new audiences. Whether through creator-driven campaigns or unexpected collaborations with other brands, the key is aligning the partnership with your brand's personality, values, and voice.

Thought Starter >
Who can you partner with that shares a similar audience? Think of a few brands you admire that have similar energy as your brand (but don't sell the same products).

## Key Takeaways from Chapter Five

1. **Choose Your Channels Intentionally:** Instead of trying to use every available platform, focus on the ones that align with your audience while staying true to what defines you as a brand.

2. **Balance Paid and Organic Efforts:** While paid media can help boost visibility, balance it with earned and owned media that builds trust and organic engagement, ensuring a well-rounded approach to amplifying your Brand Universe.

3. **Create Content That Captivates:** Your content should do more than inform—it should entertain, engage, and reflect your brand's personality. The best content reinforces your brand POV while sparking curiosity and connection.

4. **Events as Brand Showcases:** Transform your brand into a tangible experience with immersive events or activations that reflect your brand point-of-view, whether large-scale spectacles or smaller community-driven interactions.

5. **PR Stunts That Make Statements:** Bold, unexpected PR stunts create buzz and reinforce your brand's unique identity, sparking conversation, and leaving a lasting impression on your audience.

6. **Partnerships That Extend Your World:** Forge collaborations with creators, influencers, or brands that complement your POV or offer unexpected synergies. These partnerships not only expand your audience but also create fresh opportunities to infuse creativity, deepen engagement, and add new dimensions to your Brand Universe.

# 6

# Genuine Culture

If a brand's identity is the core of the universe—its center-of-gravity—culture is the matter that exists between the layers, energetically connecting them together. In recent years, the conversation around brand culture—particularly through the lens of creating a Brand Universe—has shifted toward the importance of cultural alignment and authenticity. More than ever, successful brands aren't just defined by what they sell or what they say but by the connection they foster with their communities through shared values, beliefs, and experiences.

Brand culture is not a marketing tool but a reflection of a company's internal and external actions. It's a mix of intangible elements (values and beliefs) and observable behaviors (symbols, language, and gestures). The key to creating a lasting, impactful culture is to move beyond surface-level perks and to cultivate something that resonates deeply with both employees and customers. In this chapter, we'll explore what makes an authentic brand culture and how companies like Patagonia, Zappos, and Sneaker Freaker have successfully aligned their internal cultures with their external brand image to create something truly unique and memorable.

## Cultivating an Authentic Culture

An authentic brand culture can't be faked. In fact, it's not something that is manufactured at all—it's cultivated over time through the daily actions and behaviors of the people who live and breathe it. Culture can be described as the energy your brand evokes in both your team and your customers. Too often, businesses think they can generate culture through amp'd up break rooms or superficial team-building activities. But brands that have successfully fostered genuine cultures don't focus on gimmicks like ping-pong tables, pizza lunches, or casual Fridays. They cultivate a set of beliefs and values that everyone—employees, customers, and even partners—can rally behind. It's about emotional resonance and shared meaning, not just about perks or formal programming.

*Culture isn't manufactured—it's cultivated over time through the daily actions and behaviors of the people who live and breathe it.*

A brand's culture is the accumulation of countless small decisions and interactions. It's embedded in every touchpoint, from the way employees relate to each other to how they engage with customers. Every detail, no matter how minor, contributes to the larger picture. Brands that try to force culture through one-off initiatives often find that these efforts fall flat. Instead, it's the consistency of behaviors—those daily rituals, shared beliefs, and communal habits—that slowly build the fabric of a brand's culture.

Take Zappos as an example. Renowned for its quirky, customer-first approach, Zappos' culture is embedded in every aspect of the company. The e-commerce retailer has initiatives like its Fungineering Team, which is dedicated to creating memorable, unique employee experiences, beyond the usual company lore, leaving a lasting "only Zappos would do that" impression. Those experiences include a Weird Talent Show, an event that is less about showcasing talent than displaying team member's quirkiness. The brand even has an unconventional way to attract talent that will fit their existing culture by asking potential job candidates "How weird are you on a scale of 1 to 10?" Zappos fosters an internal culture that promotes individuality, encouraging everyone to celebrate their uniqueness. These initiatives are not just internal—they spill over into the way Zappos interacts with its customers—creating a seamless cultural experience.

A vibrant culture feels alive—you can sense the energy the moment you step into the room or interact with someone from the brand. It's the unspoken understanding between employees, customers, and partners that they're part of something bigger. Brands with hollow cultures, on the other hand, may have expertly written core values displayed on their websites but lack the emotional depth that makes their values tangible. The difference lies in how much the culture is genuinely lived and felt on a day-to-day basis. A vibrant culture is full of authentic passion and purpose, while a hollow culture can feel like a set of empty promises—a veneer of values with no substance behind them.

Thought Starter >

What is one organic habit, action, or behavior you've observed from your team that energizes them? It can be something small—an inside joke that everyone seems to be in on, or a unique way they interact with each other. Can you foster this organic behavior into a team dynamic? Take inspiration from brands like Zappos, where the team members' willingness to display their quirkiness became a prerequisite for new hires.

## Internal vs. External Culture

For a brand to succeed, its culture must be aligned both internally and externally. A consistent culture across both dimensions builds a strong, recognizable brand that audiences can trust and rally behind.

Internally, culture is the foundation for how your external audience experiences your brand. Employees are often the first ambassadors of a brand's culture, and if they don't feel connected to its values, this disconnection will ripple into customer interactions. Internal culture is about more than hiring—although recruiting people who share your values is a great first step. It's about creating an environment where every team member feels invested in the brand's mission and identity.

*Strong brands are built on cultures where teams and customers share the same values.*

Patagonia is a prime example of how this alignment works. Their commitment to environmental activism isn't just something they market to customers—it's embedded deeply within their internal practices. Employees are encouraged to take part in environmental campaigns, the company offers paid time off for activism, and sustainability is prioritized in everything from product design to daily operations. This internal commitment strengthens Patagonia's external messaging, allowing them to form genuine connections with both team members and customers who share similar values.

Many companies make the mistake of focusing only on the top-down enforcement of cultural values. Traditional businesses often rely on vertical agreements that dictate employee behavior from the top. While these are necessary, they are not sufficient to build a cohesive culture. The most successful cultures also have *shared team agreements* —whether unspoken or explicit within teams—that unify people around a purpose. These agreements are less about enforcing rules and more about a *culture code*, agreeing to work together toward a common goal. When everyone is on the same page, living out the brand's values, the brand culture feels seamless, creating a unified experience for both employees and customers.

## Prompt: Draft Your Own Culture Code

Gather your team members to write their own *culture code*—a pledge between team members to work toward a common goal and to create the right environment they want to work in while pursuing the vision of the brand.

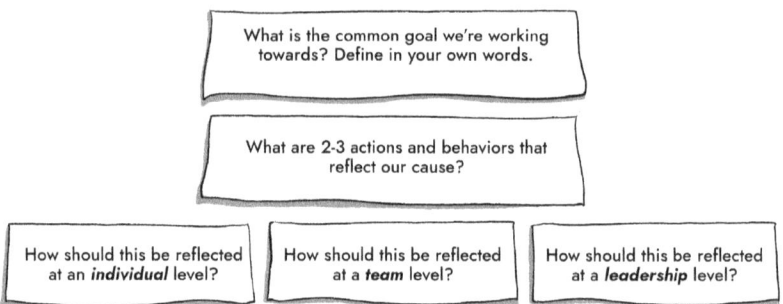

## Where to Build an Online Community

While traditional social media channels like Instagram, Facebook, and TikTok are great for introducing your brand world to a broader audience, they may not be the most effective platforms for fostering engaged communities. On these platforms, interactions are fleeting, and brands must constantly initiate conversations for any meaningful dialogue to occur. Not to mention, the competition for attention is fierce, with audiences just as easily drawn to your competitors' content as they are to yours.

One of the biggest challenges with building a community on social media is that engagement is brand-initiated and primarily one-way. Audiences aren't captive—they're scrolling through endless streams of content. As Zoe Scaman points out in her report "The New Landscape of Loyalty," traditional social platforms are "trapped in the throes of the attention economy," prioritizing broadcasting to the masses over genuine peer-to-peer interaction. This creates an environment focused more on grabbing attention than building deeper connections.

*Build your brand's community on platforms designed for engagement, not just attention.*

With the increasing limitations of social media—ranging from algorithmic restrictions to the lack of real community-building opportunities—brands have turned to new platforms designed specifically for fostering engaged, niche communities. Platforms like Circle, WhatsApp, Discord, and Mighty Networks have emerged as spaces where peer-to-peer engagement, co-creation, and shared value thrive. These platforms allow brands to cultivate deeper relationships with their audience, creating a sense of membership and belonging rather than passive following.

LEGO, for example, has embraced Discord to create a community space where users can discuss everything from set designs to fan-made creations. LEGO's Discord servers are more than just a space for conversation—they're hubs of co-creation, where people can actively share their own ideas, participate in discussions, and engage with other like-minded individuals. This approach fosters a stronger sense of community ownership and deeper brand loyalty as fans become active participants in the LEGO Universe rather than just consumers. Niche community platforms also provide space for co-creation, giving audiences the opportunity to shape and contribute to the brand's Universe. For example, e.l.f. Cosmetics has used Discord to host real-time chats and product discussions, allowing their community to contribute ideas and feedback. This level of co-creation builds a sense of ownership and fosters a closer bond between brand and audience.

What sets these platforms apart from traditional social media is their focus on building long-term, meaningful relationships. By allowing brands to facilitate genuine conversations, these platforms offer opportunities for brands to immerse themselves in the cultural landscapes of their audience, creating a deeper, lasting connection.

## How Subcultures Influence Your Brand Universe

While only a few brands have the power to spark entirely new cultural movements, a more accessible strategy is to tap into existing subcultures. Brands that successfully embed themselves in subcultures go beyond simply adopting surface-level identifiers like slang, clothing, or lifestyle trends. To truly connect with a subculture, brands must take the time to understand the deeper layers—the values, behaviors, and emotional drivers that shape how people within those cultures think and act.

Subcultures are often defined by their distinct beliefs, priorities, and rituals. What sets brands apart in these spaces is their ability to listen and learn from the people within these communities, gaining insight into the underlying motivations behind their actions. For example, in the world of gaming, it's not just about the types of games played or the platforms used but also about the unique ways players interact with each other—and even individual expression within virtual spaces. Understanding this allows brands to create products, experiences, or campaigns that resonate on a deeper level, instead of relying on superficial markers.

*Brands that authentically engage with subcultures become part of their ecosystem.*

Take Sneaker Freaker, a brand that began as a small publication serving the niche world of sneaker enthusiasts, otherwise known as "sneakerheads." From the beginning, Sneaker Freaker wasn't just reporting on the latest shoe releases; it immersed itself in the authentic experience of sneaker culture. The brand understood that for sneakerheads, sneakers were more than just articles of clothing or collectibles; they were part of a larger cultural conversation that touched on art, identity, and self-expression. Over time, by staying true to the community's values and authentically engaging with the deeper meaning behind sneaker culture, Sneaker Freaker didn't just reflect the culture—it helped shape it.

Sneaker Freaker's editor, Simon "Woody" Wood, is recognized as an authentic ambassador within sneaker culture, someone who wasn't just capitalizing on a trend but who lived and breathed it. Woody's deep involvement and understanding of the sneakerhead mindset—valuing limited releases, celebrating the artistry behind custom designs, and diving into the history and nuances of sneaker production—solidified Sneaker Freaker's place not just as an observer but as an authority in the space. Today, Sneaker Freaker is a global force, with the brand having helped shape conversations around sneaker design, authenticity, and value, all while maintaining a deep connection with the community that birthed it.

Image: sneakerfreaker.com

By fully immersing in subcultures, brands can tap into powerful emotional connections and become integral parts of these worlds. Rather than imposing your brand's message onto a subculture, it's about becoming a conduit for their world and allowing their values and stories to flow through your brand. When a brand authentically understands and values the core elements of a subculture, it becomes part of the community's ecosystem, fostering a sense of belonging among its members.

Whether it's niche subcultures like sneakerheads, underground music scenes, or broader movements (like environmental activism), aligning with subcultures adds depth and richness to your Brand Universe. It allows your brand to go beyond transactional interactions and instead create an ecosystem centered around values and experiences. Brands that embrace this approach foster a deeper connection with their audience, creating lasting relationships based on authenticity and respect for the subculture's core tenets.

## Prompt: Spark Your Cult(ure) Status

Think about a subculture or community that aligns with your brand. What drives this subculture beyond the superficial differences? How can your brand become a genuine participant in this community? Write down three ways your brand can immerse itself in the subculture and foster an authentic connection.

_____

_____

_____

_____

_____

## Recognizing and Rewarding Champions

Brands that successfully cultivate loyalty today understand that audiences seek more than just coupons or discounts—they want experiences, status, and opportunities to co-create within the Brand's Universe. Modern loyalty programs have evolved from accruing points to emphasizing shared values and engagement, moving beyond simple transactions. When loyalty is nurtured as a two-way relationship, it turns champions—customers, employees, or brand advocates—into active contributors to a brand's culture and community.

These loyalty programs thrive on creating a sense of adventure and meaningful challenges. For instance, Glossier's G Collective invites customers to embark on "quests" where they provide ideas and feedback, showing loyalty through engagement in exchange for insider access to new products and experiences. By encouraging champions to co-create with the brand, Glossier has turned its community into more than just a customer base—it's a collective of passionate advocates who feel directly connected to Glossier's Brand Universe.

*When loyalty is nurtured, it turns champions into active contributors to your brand's culture.*

Similarly, The North Face's XPLR Pass is built around the brand's culture of adventure and environmental stewardship. Through the XPLR Pass, loyal customers gain access to limited-edition releases, product testing, and curated experiences—like guided outdoor adventures. This loyalty model goes beyond perks; it offers fans a chance to embody the brand's values in ways that deepen their relationship with the North Face community. Brands can also use loyalty programs to reward employees. The key is to think beyond rewarding performance to recognize employees that embody your brand values. Cyclocross, a distributor of bike parts and accessories, has a program for team members that aligns with its values of environmental consciousness. Employees who bike, carpool, or use public transportation to work are rewarded with financial incentives. This practice not only reinforces Cyclocross's brand values but also builds an internal culture that employees feel proud to champion.

Thought Starter >

What "quests" or challenges could you offer that align with your brand's values, prompting champions to provide ideas, insights, and feedback? Use these opportunities to recognize contributors with unique perks that go beyond the transactional, building deeper loyalty through shared experiences and achievements.

## The Dangers of a Toxic Culture

Even the most immersive Brand Universe can unravel if it's built on a toxic foundation. Culture can either elevate a brand, aligning employees and customers around shared values, or it can erode it from within. For brands that project a positive image externally, any internal misalignment can be catastrophic—potentially undermining years of brand building. A strong brand can never fully compensate for a fractured culture, and a toxic workplace can damage even the most successful brands, sometimes beyond repair.

A brand that fosters an unhealthy internal culture will eventually reveal its cracks. Toxicity can seep into public perception, eroding trust and loyalty. Brands must work to ensure that internal values align with external promises, or they risk being exposed and dismantled. Building a Brand Universe that thrives on authenticity requires consistency between the way a brand operates internally and the values it projects to the world. Translation: Walk the walk, don't just talk the talk.

*A toxic culture doesn't stay hidden—it seeps into public perception and damages your brand.*

The Wing, a women-focused community and co-working space, offers a recent example of how a misaligned internal culture can cause a brand to collapse. The brand experience for The Wing was meticulously crafted—from the iconic design of its spaces to the top-tier programming with prominent feminist voices. As a member of The Wing's Los Angeles location, I personally experienced the company's on-point branding and immersive environment, which felt like a dream brand world for women professionals. But beneath the well-designed surface, cracks began to show. When former employees exposed issues of mistreatment and a lack of inclusivity, it became clear that the internal culture didn't match The Wing's external messaging.

Despite its impressive brand experience, the internal misalignment—exacerbated by the challenges of a global pandemic—ultimately led to its downfall, highlighting how essential it is for a brand's internal culture to reflect its external values. This misalignment is a critical vulnerability as people are the heart of any Brand Universe. Even one individual with toxic behaviors can damage morale, alienate teams, and, over time, compromise the entire brand culture. It's essential to set boundaries, hire slow, and fire fast to protect the community you've built.

Communicating your brand values should go beyond marketing—they need to resonate internally and serve as genuine guides for the company. Tying values to specific stories or experiences can make them more meaningful, giving employees a sense of shared purpose that strengthens culture from within.

## Key Takeaways from Chapter Six

1. **Align Internal and External Culture:** Build a consistent culture that reflects your brand's values both internally among employees and externally with customers.

2. **Infuse Values with Meaning:** Bring your brand's values to life by tying them to stories and daily actions that resonate with your team. These narratives create a shared sense of purpose, deepening emotional connections with both employees and customers.

3. **Tap into Subcultures to Deepen Connection:** Align with subcultures that reflect your brand's values by understanding their unique beliefs, rituals, and emotional drivers. Engaging authentically with these communities fosters loyalty and integrates your brand into their cultural ecosystem.

4. **Recognize and Reward Champions:** Build loyalty by celebrating employees and customers who embody your brand's values with incentives that reward engagement and reinforce cultural alignment.

5. **Address Toxicity Early:** A toxic culture doesn't remain hidden—it leaks into public perception, eroding trust and loyalty. Set boundaries, hire slow, and act decisively to protect the integrity of your brand world.

# Conclusion

A Brand Universe is an immersive world, built from a distinct point-of-view and amplified by experiences that resonate deeply with those who connect with it. It's a space where emotional connection, shared values, and unique brand touchpoints combine to create something unforgettable. A truly impactful brand world offers a rich, dimensional experience that gives people more than just a product; it offers them a chance to be part of something meaningful.

## Putting Principles into Action

Creating a Brand Universe isn't about following a formula but embracing foundational principles that you can apply flexibly, no matter the size or stage of your business. Whether you're refining your point-of-view, developing a distinct brand language, crafting unique experiences, amplifying your identity to draw audiences in, or cultivating a genuine culture, every touchpoint adds to the layers in your brand world. These aren't one-time actions; they're ongoing and iterative, intended to adapt as your brand grows. As you build and refine the layers of your Brand Universe, focus on intimate and memorable touchpoints that create lasting loyalty and community.

## Embracing the Role of Your Audience as Co-Creators

A Brand Universe thrives on connection and collaboration. Rather than dictating every aspect of your brand, allow your audience to co-create with you. The most resonant brands invite people to help shape the brand's ever-evolving story, adding authenticity to make the experience more relevant. Your audience can enhance your brand in ways that top-down strategies never could. Lean into that collaboration—it's this collective energy that will amplify your brand's reach and credibility.

## The Power of Clarity, Confidence, and Consistency

As you build, stay grounded in your brand POV, with confidence in your vision and consistency in your brand's expression. Clarity helps your brand resonate with the right people, confidence enables you to make bold, aligned decisions, and consistency allows your audience to develop trust and familiarity with you. While the details of your brand may evolve, these principles should guide each step, helping your Brand Universe stay true to itself even as it grows and adapts.

## Brand Building as a Journey

Building a brand world is an ongoing journey, one that involves continuous learning, adjusting, and experimenting. Your Brand Universe is a living entity that will change with time, feedback, and new insights. Let this book be a companion on that journey, a source you can revisit as you face new challenges and opportunities in your brand-building process. As you move forward, embrace each challenge as an opportunity to deepen the connection with your audience and evolve the world you're creating.

## A Call to Boldness and Creativity

Ultimately, a Brand Universe isn't just about standing out—it's about standing for something. Whether you're a founder or a marketer, remember that every choice you make, big or small, shapes the brand's future. Continue to experiment, invest in the emotional and narrative aspects of your brand, and engage deeply with your audience. Approach your brand with intentionality, designing each element as a meaningful step in your Brand Universe. By staying committed to your unique vision, you'll create a Brand Universe that not only resonates but also endures.

# About the Author

With a dynamic 18-year career weaving together strategy and storytelling across roles in market research, fashion, brand copywriting, and customer experience, Robyn Young brings a holistic perspective as a brand strategist and founder of Young & Co., a creative brand partner for next-gen trailblazers.

Known for building magnetic brands that turn customers into loyal fans, Robyn draws on her real-world entrepreneurial experience—and an active role in over 70 brand launches—to help founders and teams uncover a distinct identity and craft compelling ways to amplify it. Her clients range from bootstrapping entrepreneurs to fast-growing innovators, market disruptors, and established enterprises, all united by a desire to create legacies with their brands.

As a seasoned speaker and workshop lead, Robyn has shared her insights on brand-building nationwide, empowering businesses to find clarity, confidence, and a resonant voice. Her creative vision has helped clients secure over $100M in revenue, boost sales, increase customer loyalty, and solidify their brand identities.

In her personal life, Robyn is a mixed media artist and improv enthusiast who believes that creative expression is the gift each of us has to connect with the world—a philosophy she applies to her work every day. Robyn currently lives in Pasadena, CA, with her husband and daughter.

**Contact Robyn for interviews, speaking or project inquiries.**

Email: robyn@robynyoung.co
Website: www.robynyoung.co
LinkedIn: www.linkedin.com/in/robyn-young
TikTok: www.tiktok.com/@robynyoung.co

# Did You Enjoy this Book?

If you enjoyed reading this book, you can help by suggesting it to someone else you think might like it, and **please leave a positive review** wherever you purchased it. This does a lot in helping others find the book. We thank you in advance for taking a few moments to do this.

*THANK YOU*

www.ingramcontent.com/pod-product-compliance
Lightning Source LLC
Chambersburg PA
CBHW051318120626
46547CB00015B/2299